CORPORATE AND FAMILY GOVERNANCE

The two disciplines that carry family businesses across generations

Christos Christou

Clink Street

Published by Clink Street Publishing 2022

ISBNs:
978-1-914498-82-4 - paperback
978-1-914498-83-1 - ebook

CORPORATE AND FAMILY GOVERNANCE

The two disciplines that carry family
businesses across generations

Dedicated to my family and friends

Acknowledgments

I have been interested in Corporate Governance since my days as a banker with the European Bank for Reconstruction and Development in the 1990s and in family governance since my days as a private equity investor in Central Europe in the early 2000s. An assignment undertaken on behalf of the European Bank for Reconstruction and Development in 2014 gave me the opportunity to codify much of what is covered in this book. This assignment, completed over 18 months and 12 visits to Tunisia, introduced and implemented Corporate Governance to the holdings of the Slama family and introduced Family Governance to the family itself. I would, therefore, like to acknowledge Ghassen Slama and his family for their foresight in seeking to introduce Corporate Governance in their family's holdings and for trusting me to assist them on this journey.

The book itself has come about as a result of encouragement I have received from respected and trusted friends including Doug Peel, whose early encouragement played a catalytic role, Per Frost whose observations, particularly on strategy and culture have informed the relevant subchapters, Ben Johnson, Marios Nicolettis, Spyros Papas, Dave Jordan, Rytis Jakaitis and last but not least Marco Luchini who has also been a trusted advisor on this and other matters since our college days. Special mention and thanks are also reserved for Alejandro Marchionna-Fare, a friend of many years who is similarly committed to good governance in all its guises. They have all contributed with their early review of the online presence of Family Governance Associates and early draft of this book. And Charles Beauduin whose exemplary commitment to innovation inspired the relevant sub-chapter. I am grateful for their friendship and their contributions.

It is inevitable that a book like this is based partly on experiences and partly on values and interests of the author. These experiences, values and interests do not develop overnight but rather reflect both one's early beginnings and one's life trajectory to the point of writing. I would thus like to also acknowledge and register my thanks and gratitude to my parents Andreas and Koulla, my sister Lena, my wife Sonja and my daughters Alexandra and Andriana, as well as my extended family of uncles, aunts, cousins, nephews and nieces. I would also like to acknowledge and register my thanks to all the friends that I have been fortunate to make over the years. Their friendship has been a blessing and my conversations with them a source of wisdom.

Foreword

Corporate Governance is an essential ingredient in the wellbeing of companies and by extension, economies. In its absence, or when practiced poorly, the risk of company failure increases significantly.

In many countries, companies are required to comply with specific codes of Corporate Governance. The requirements placed on companies by these codes are often linked to the size of the companies concerned. In the case of listed companies, compliance with the relevant code of Corporate Governance is expected by capital providers and other stakeholders.

When companies fail, their failures are sometimes attributed to noncompliance with specific aspects of Corporate Governance or even aspects of governance that were not sufficiently covered by the existing Corporate Governance Codes. Consequently, high profile company failures can sometimes lead to reviews and updates of existing codes of Corporate Governance with the intention of minimizing the risk of future failures. It follows that Corporate Governance is a discipline which is dynamic and constantly evolving.

Many businesses, both private and listed, are family owned. The longevity of such businesses is linked to good Corporate Governance as well as the practice of Family Governance, which allows the business and the family to interact in ways that are mutually beneficial.

The author is keen to promote both good Corporate Governance and Family Governance. He has developed and compiled a number of resources in a site that is intended to promote Corporate Governance and Family Governance www.familygovernanceassociates.com This book summarizes the most critical elements of Corporate Governance and Family Governance in a general setting and is intended as a primer on these topics.

London 2022

Table of Contents

Introduction

This book is divided into five chapters. Chapter 1 addresses Corporate Governance and seeks to explain what it is, why it is important and how to introduce it in a corporate setting. Moreover it seeks to provide primers on some of the key ingredients of Good Corporate Governance.

Chapter 2 addresses failures in Corporate Governance and draws lessons learnt from such failures. It is clear from the study of such failures, that the imperative of good Corporate Governance is true irrespective of who owns the affected entity. Corporate Governance failures occur with disastrous consequences in privately-held, family-controlled as well as listed entities and even government-controlled entities. The case studies presented in this chapter are all selected on the basis of their relevance as well as the extensive attention they have attracted by the press or relevant regulators and in some cases the courts; any associated litigation and regulators' investigations have ran their course with reports of what went wrong widely and publicly available, appeal processes completed and sentences served. The chronology of events and the facts of the cases, including behaviours of key actors in them presented in this chapter are based on publicly available information and reports.

Chapter 3 focuses on family businesses which account for a very significant part of economic activity around the world. Beyond identifying the key parameters characterizing family businesses, this chapter also seeks to codify the ways families interact with the businesses they control. It is only through understanding the scope and nature of such interactions that one can hope to introduce family governance arrangements that will regulate such interactions.

Chapter 4 focuses on Family Governance and seeks to explain what it includes, why it is important and how to introduce it. It further provides primers on some of the key aspects of Family Governance.

The final chapter seeks to draw conclusions and explains how good Corporate Governance and Family Governance are both necessary ingredients for a family business to stand a chance of becoming a multigenerational business.

Inevitably a book is defined by what it includes and what it does not include and by what it emphasizes and what it does not. I believe that this book has covered all the main ingredients of Corporate Governance and Family Governance and is in that sense complete. However, I also freely acknowledge that the topics of Corporate Governance and Family Governance as well as each of their subtopics merit entire books on their own. Nowhere is this truer than the subtopic of Environmental Social Governance (ESG) which has become a major consideration in recent times, particularly for listed companies. The word "primer" used to describe the level of exposition that is provided for each subtopic in this book is thus advisedly selected.

The structure of this book mirrors, to a degree, the structure and resources available on the site www.familygovernanceassociates.com. Although the book can be seen as a companion piece to the site, it is intended to be a standalone resource in itself.

Chapter 1:
Corporate Governance

1.1. Definition, importance and introduction of Corporate Governance

What is Corporate Governance?

The usual textbook definition of Corporate Governance refers to the prescription of rules of engagement between

- ✓ owners as providers of capital
- ✓ managers as executors of business strategy with owners' capital and
- ✓ directors as formulators of strategy and supervisors of managers but answerable to owners

Schematically, Corporate Governance is often presented as a set of bilateral relationships in a triangle linking owners, managers and directors.

Figure 1.1.a. Traditional Corporate Governance Triangular Relationships

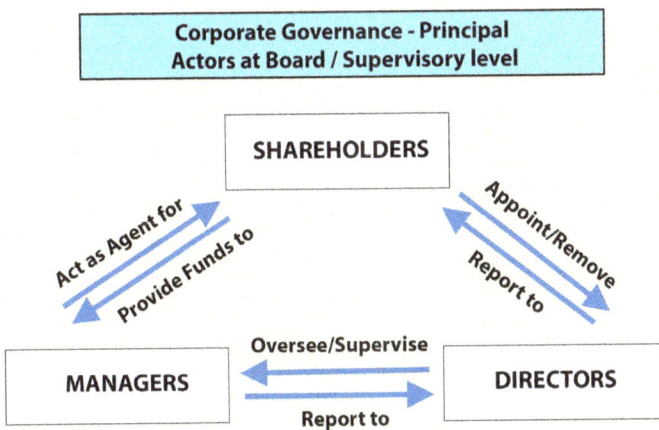

This definition is clearly concerned with agency issues and is seen from the perspective of owners who may not always be involved in the business.

Below the shareholder level, Corporate Governance also acts as an umbrella concept and focuses among other things on the interaction of planning, allocation and monitoring as illustrated below.

Figure 1.1.b. Corporate Governance framework with Culture as a key ingredient

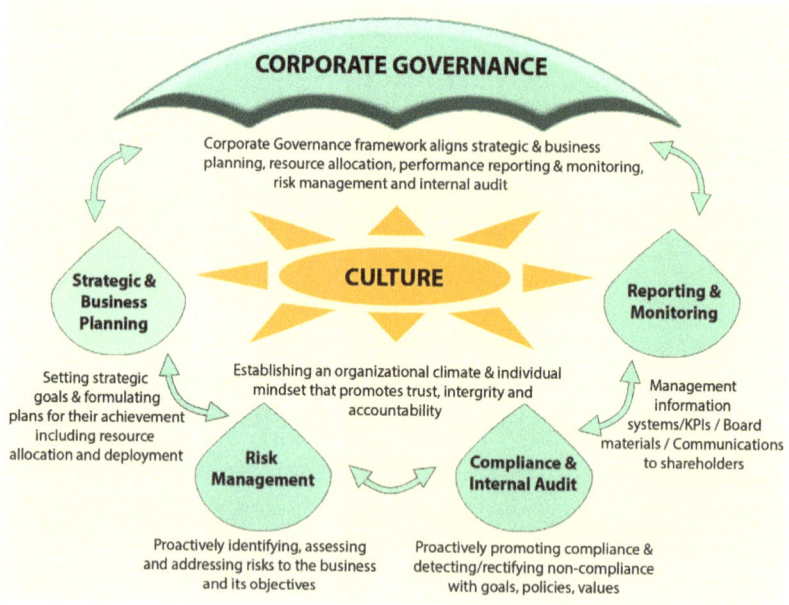

In this broader definition, Corporate Governance pertains to structures, processes and culture for the **direction** and **control** of companies. It concerns the relationships among the management, the management oversight body (usually the Board of Directors, sometimes substituted or supplemented by a Supervisory Board), controlling shareholders, minority shareholders and other stakeholders.

Direction means **all** the decisions that relate to setting the overall strategic direction of the company such as:

- ✓ Long term strategic decisions including large scale investment decisions
- ✓ Mergers and acquisitions
- ✓ Succession planning and appointment of senior managers.

Control means **all** the actions necessary to oversee management's performance and follow-up on the implementation of the strategic decisions already taken.

All in all, good Corporate Governance can be understood as an adequate system of checks and balances in all the dimensions that can impact the survival and prosperity of a business. And poor Corporate Governance can be understood as an inadequate or failing system of checks and balances that exposes the business to risks that can threaten its very survival, let alone its prosperity.

Why does Corporate Governance matter?

Good Corporate Governance ensures a clear definition of the role, duties, rights and expectations of each of a company's governing bodies.

It follows that good Corporate Governance confers benefits on the business as it promotes conditions that are conducive to sustainable development of the business and improve its resilience to shocks and challenges, thus also enhancing its longevity. The absence or failure of Corporate Governance undermines a company's resilience and can therefore increase the risks of business distress and failure.

Following high profile business failures attributed or linked to Corporate Governance failings or shortcomings, many countries have introduced mandatory codes of Corporate Governance as a form of pre-emptive safeguarding. In many jurisdictions listed companies not only have to adhere to the relevant code of Corporate Governance, but they also have to report publicly on their compliance. Capital providers such as banks and institutional investors are increasingly mindful of companies' records on Corporate Governance and those with poor records can find their access to capital is negatively affected. Conversely, companies with good records of Corporate Governance are rewarded by better market ratings and greater access to capital including access to capital at more favourable terms and conditions. This is becoming increasingly the case as in recent years the term Environmental Social Governance (ESG) has become a byword for investment criteria used by socially conscious investors in listed companies. Such investors are interested in companies'

- ✓ stewardship of nature, hence the term Environmental
- ✓ relationships with stakeholders such as clients, suppliers, employees and local communities where a company operates, hence the term Social
- ✓ Corporate Governance practices, hence the term Governance.

Arguably good Corporate Governance, which is aimed at ensuring the prosperity and longevity of companies, includes adopting sustainable business models and practices. In a broad sense, responsible stewardship of nature and balanced relationships with stakeholders are to a large extent manifestations of good Corporate Governance. The opposite is also true. Irresponsible stewardship of nature and predatory relationships with stakeholders are symptoms of absence or failures in Corporate Governance which can undermine a company's prosperity and longevity. Nevertheless, in spelling out Environmental and Social in their investment criteria alongside Governance, socially conscious investors help remind Boards, particularly of listed companies, of their broader responsibilities.

1.2.   The dynamic nature of Corporate Governance

It is evident that the challenges, risks and opportunities that a company faces are linked to its stage of evolution.

A start-up typically faces the challenge of marshalling sufficient resources, including financial and human resources, in a way that will allow it to become viable in a self-sustaining way. Availability and scarcity of resources are often key challenges and risk factors and there is never a guarantee that a start-up will make it.

An established company that is very profitable and has a strong balance sheet, faces the very different challenge of deploying its plentiful resources, including financial and human resources, in ways that maintain its strong position and take advantage of opportunities without exposing the business to undue risk.

In between these two rather extreme examples, there are companies which face their own version of the challenge of how to marshal and deploy resources in pursuit of opportunities whilst at the same time managing risks, including the risk of failure.

In addition to the stage of evolution and financial condition of the business, the ownership structure of a business is also an important factor affecting the interplay between marshalling resources, pursuing opportunities and managing risk. So, whereas a start-up may have a limited set of owners or shareholders, some of whom at least will be actively involved in the business, an established company listed on a major exchange will have thousands or even millions of shareholders with very little direct involvement in the business.

Clearly the nature of the ownership and the stage of the evolution of the business are often linked. Both are dynamic. They are also both factors that affect the nature of Corporate Governance that is appropriate and relevant for a business. Corporate Governance does **not** come in one size that fits all. It is much more a case of horses for courses. And to the degree a business is dynamic and evolves, so too should its Corporate Governance arrangements be dynamic and evolve in order to remain relevant and effective.

1.3. Constituent elements of Corporate Governance

Corporate Governance comprises of a number of elements that merit description and discussion in the primers that follow. A very important element is the oversight that is exercised on a company and there are a number of characteristics that define such oversight, each of which deserve a sub-chapter of their own, including:

- ✓ The type of oversight body oversight body that ensure adequate monitoring of executive management takes place. This oversight can be exercised via a single Board structure historically associated with the United Kingdom and United States or a two-tier Board structure historically associated with Germany. The two approaches are described below
- ✓ The role and responsibilities of the Board of Directors
- ✓ The materials that should be made available to a Board of Directors in order to facilitate decision-making and the exercise of oversight
- ✓ The composition of the Board of Directors, similarly in order to facilitate decision-making and the exercise of oversight

Another element is Risk Management which when practiced properly safeguards the company's assets, prospects and longevity without sacrificing its potential and growth.

A third element is the Internal Audit Function (IAF) that acts as the eyes and ears of an oversight body.

A fourth one are the Management Information Systems (MIS) and Key Performance Indicators (KPIs) that are introduced in order to aid decision-making the exercise of timely and effective oversight.

A further element which obviously constitutes part of Corporate Governance is the Code of Conduct a company adopts in order to establish its own rules of engagement with internal and external parties.

An element which is less obvious but no less important part of Corporate Governance is the strategy review cycle and its link to the company's choices when it comes to innovation, since Strategy and Innovation concern choices by the oversight body of any company and such choices are made with the company's longevity and prosperity in mind.

Last but not least, is Culture, as we have already described in the definitional diagram 1.1. Corporate Governance Framework with Culture as a key ingredient.

1.3.1. Approaches to oversight body and its function

At shareholder level, Corporate Governance deals with the arrangements under which oversight is exercised on the management and affairs of the company on behalf of its owners. There are two principal approaches that inform these arrangements:

   a. the two-tier oversight approach, which is historically associated with Germany and adopted in a number of countries in Europe including Austria, Finland and Sweden and in China
   b. the unitary oversight body approach, which is associated with the United Kingdom and United States and has been adopted in many other countries

In many countries, Corporate Governance codes are used to guide companies on what constitutes appropriate governance arrangements. The relevant Corporate Governance codes for specific countries can be downloaded from the European Corporate Governance Institute (ECGI) www.ecgi.com, an international non-profit association providing, a forum for debate and dialogue between academics, legislators and practitioners, and focusing on major Corporate Governance issues. See: www.ecgi.global/content/codes

1.3.1.1. The two-tier Board oversight structure

Under this approach, there are two separate Boards, an Executive Board or Management Board for day-to-day business and a Supervisory Board elected by shareholders and in some countries also employees, for appointing and supervising the Executive or Management Board. Oversight is exercised by the two separate Boards.

The Supervisory Board is chaired by the Chairman of the Company and is usually made up of non-executives, though in some jurisdictions it can include employee representatives. Generally, the Supervisory Board guides and monitors the Management Board. The Supervisory Board is also involved in long-term strategic planning.

The Management Board is made up exclusively of executives and is led by the Chief Executive Officer (CEO) of the company. It meets frequently, often weekly, to deal with operational issues. Some contracting decisions and strategic planning decisions may have to be approved by the Supervisory Board.

The two Boards have to cooperate closely in developing the business strategy through a steady flow of information between them. The information flow normally includes Risk Management, business development and any deviations from initially agreed plans. Open discussions between members of the two Boards are also vital for the functionality of the business under the dual Board management system as the Boards must exchange information frequently.

Figure 1.3.1.1.a. Dual Board oversight structure

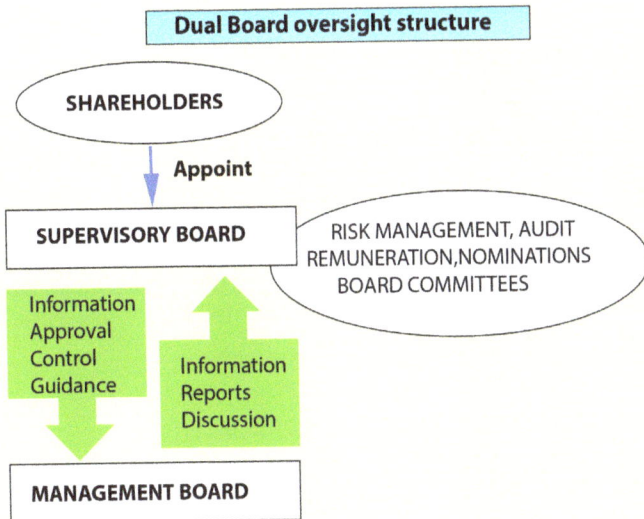

What is Codetermination ?

The dual Board system is closely associated with Germany as it was introduced there in the 19th century. Since 1976, under German law, workers have the right to participate in the management of the companies they work for by electing representatives (usually trade union representatives) to the Supervisory Board of Directors. In companies with more than 2,000 employees, such employee representatives may make up almost half the Supervisory Board and in companies with 500 to 2,000 employees, employee representatives make up a third of the Supervisory Board. This employee participation is called "*Codetermination*" and clearly contributes to better information sharing and to building trust between employees and their companies and managers which can lead to relatively peaceful industrial relations. On the other hand, decision making can be slower though some studies, notably in Sweden, have suggested efficiency improved with worker representation.

Figure 1.3.1.1.b. German Dual Board incorporating Co-determination

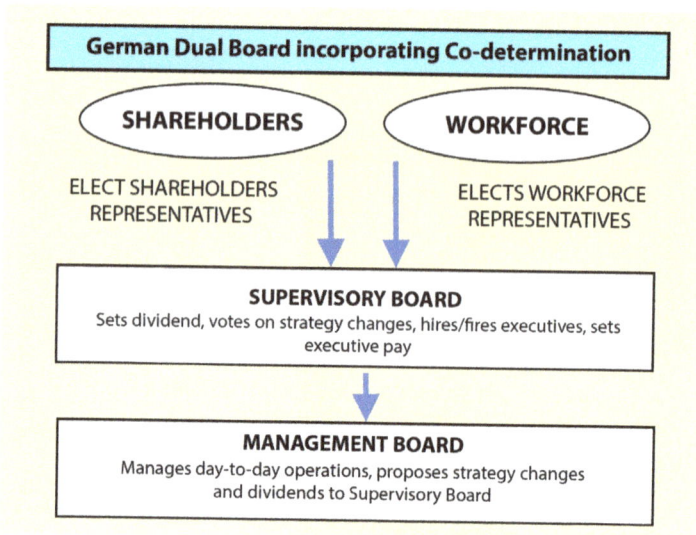

1.3.1.2. The unitary Board oversight structure

Under this approach, there is only one oversight body, the Board of Directors, which is comprised of both executives of the company and non-executives. In the United Kingdom, since the early 1990s following the recommendations of the Cadbury Report in 1992, the roles of Chairman and CEO are held by two different people. In the United States, the role of Chairman and CEO can be combined and very often one person holds both posts, but there is a trend towards splitting the role. So, there are in effect two variants of the unitary Board structure – the British variant and the American variant.

Figure 1.3.1.2.a.UK and US Variants of Unitary Board structure

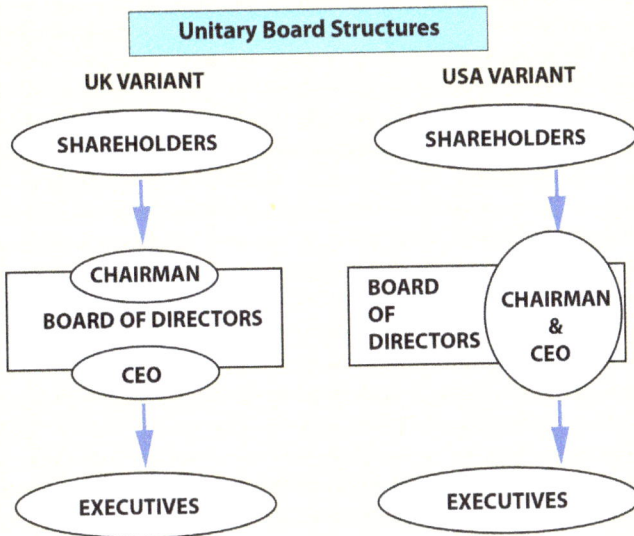

1.3.1.3. Comparison between unitary and dual Board structures

There are arguments in favour of each of the approaches and variants. Proponents and adherents of the dual Board approach point to the clear distinction it ensures between management by the Executive Board and governance by the Supervisory Board which in their view allows clearer lines of authority. The aim is to prevent a conflict of interest and too much power being concentrated in the hands of one person. Some acknowledge a strong parallel of the dual Board approach with the structure of government, which tends to separate the political cabinet, ultimately accountable to voters who elect the parties that form such a cabinet, from the management oriented civil service that acts according to the directions of the cabinet. Using a two-tier system might also result in more monitoring and less aggressive performance targets, particularly where employees are strongly represented in the Supervisory Board. Critics of the dual Board approach suggest that financial efficiency may be impeded by reduced communication and the higher costs of running two Boards.

Proponents of the unitary Board approach point to lower oversight costs of having just one Board mixing executives and non-executives and also to speedier decision-making and greater flexibility in changing strategic direction, particularly in the absence of worker representatives at the Board level. Proponents of the American approach of combining the roles of Chairman and CEO, point to the powerful platform that this creates for exceptional leaders to make a big difference to the fortunes of the companies they lead. On the other hand, proponents of the British approach of splitting the Chairman and CEO roles, point to lower concentration of power in the hands of one individual and greater checks and balances that result in greater resilience.

There is no settled opinion on what structure is "best" as there are examples of excellent outcomes as well as poor outcomes under both unitary Boards and two-tier Boards. Fundamentally, such structures are simply tools in the hands of executive and non-executive directors. Ultimately it is the shareholders' and directors' responsibility to achieve good Corporate Governance whichever way they see fit given the environment in which their companies operate.

1.3.2. Board of Directors Role and Responsibilities

The Board of Directors is the body responsible for setting the strategy for the company. In order to set the strategy, the Board needs to review and evaluate present and future opportunities, threats and risks in the external environment and take into account current and future strengths, weaknesses and risks. It needs to determine and assess strategic options and select those options the pursuit of which will form the corporate strategy.

Setting the strategy is of course only the first part of the Board's responsibility with respect to setting the direction of the company. The second part of this responsibility is to determine what resources are needed to implement the corporate strategy and then secure or allocate these resources for the implementation of the chosen strategy. Thus, a Board needs to understand the company's organizational structure and capability and ensure they are appropriate for implementing the chosen strategy or strategies. The Board assesses the availability and adequacy of existing resources and allocates the appropriate resources (for example human, financial and technological resources) to support the implementation of the chosen strategy or strategies. In this context, the Board also exercises its responsibility of appointing the company's CEO and other members of the senior executive management team such as Chief Financial Officer (CFO) and Marketing Director. If deemed necessary, the Board becomes responsible for securing any incremental resources needed to ensure implementation of the strategy.

The Board is also responsible for the approval of budgets and plans that the executive management formulates and recommends for the implementation of the strategy set by the Board. Once such budgets and plans are approved by the Board, its role shifts to monitoring company and management actual performance relative to agreed targets and goals. Such monitoring needs to be timely and effective in order to facilitate timely and effective adjustments to strategy and resource allocation if necessary. Monitoring and assessing company and management performance also allows the Board to recognize and reward outperformance or address underperformance.

As the company's oversight body, a Board approves financial accounts and other regulatory submissions. It reports to shareholders and other stakeholders such as regulatory authorities and tax authorities, and is ultimately accountable to them. And it is also legally responsible for ensuring compliance with legal and regulatory requirements such as environmental regulations and health and safety regulations. In this context, proactive and transparent communications can promote goodwill towards the company from stakeholders.

By law, in the United Kingdom, Directors' duties include the duties to:

- Act within powers in accordance with the company's constitution and for the purpose they were granted these powers
- Promote the success of the company
- Exercise independent judgment
- Exercise reasonable care, skill and diligence
- Avoid conflicts of interest

- Decline any benefits from third parties
- Declare any interest in a proposed transaction or arrangement

The last, but by no means the least, function of a Board of Directors is to set the company's values, policies and standards. It does so, by formulating governance and ethics codes and ensuring they are followed. Moreover it determines the company's policies and ensures they are practiced as intended. It supports and works with the internal audit function to ensure appropriate oversight. It also supervises and ensures appropriate Risk Management processes are in place and functioning to protect the company's position. Perhaps the most powerful way through which it serves this function is the power of its example, particularly in respect of its own adherence to good Corporate Governance standards. Its actions, particularly in moments of crisis, can make or break the company.

Consider the example of the actions of the Johnson & Johnson Board in October 1982 when faced with deaths arising from the use of Tylenol tablets from bottles that appeared to have been tampered with and laced with cyanide. The Johnson & Johnson Board did not try to mitigate the cost to the company by trying to identify which batches of bottles might have been effected. Instead, with 31 million Tylenol bottles in circulation with a retail value of $100 million, it issued a nationwide recall of all Tylenol, at the cost of millions in foregone revenues and profits. The public appreciated the clear demonstration that Johnson & Johnson put the customer's welfare ahead of company profit and Tylenol not only recovered its market leading position after the incident but actually strengthened it. The values demonstrated by the Johnson & Johnson Board on how to handle the crisis became an object lesson in crisis management and cemented the company's bond of trust with customers for a generation.

1.3.3. Board of Directors Information Pack and Presentation

1.3.3.1. What is an appropriate frequency of Board meetings?

Boards discharge their duties through meetings and the resolutions they pass at such meetings. The frequency of their meetings is therefore an important parameter to consider. This frequency is a function of the industry and company circumstances and condition.

Start-ups face shifting priorities and potentially existential challenges as they grow to break even. Companies in distress face existential threats in the midst of turnaround efforts. Companies in fast moving industries face more frequent challenges and threats but also opportunities. Thus, start-ups, companies in distress and companies in fast moving industries tend to require more frequent Board meetings and may need monthly Board meetings or even more frequent meetings in periods of crises. On the other hand for dominant companies in mature markets three to four Board meetings a year may be sufficient.

1.3.3.2. The function of Board materials

The materials submitted to a Board are a means of formal communication. As such they provide information which helps Boards in their deliberations and decision-making and they need to be:

- Relevant – to the business and the issues under consideration
- Informative – improve understanding and insight
- Succinct – as concise as possible
- Clear – leave no room for misunderstanding

Thus a useful acronym to guide preparation of Board submissions from these attributes is RISC, with a C for the last attribute of clear.

The materials need to include analyses as well as outline and assess options and of course the management's recommendations for the Board's approval. Board materials are also the means by which the company's management can submit requests to the Board. Submissions to the Board are intended to improve its understanding particularly in respect of relevant market and competition issues, as well as create a common understanding between Board and management so that they can facilitate decision-making. When it comes to performance, the materials need to include follow-up on any past actions agreed.

Overall, Board materials should serve as a compass for monitoring adherence to and progress relative to plan and strategy. They also need to serve as a kind of radar and early detection mechanism to identify risks, threats and opportunities in a timely fashion.

Figure 1.3.3.2.a. Board materials as tools for charting course and identifying risks

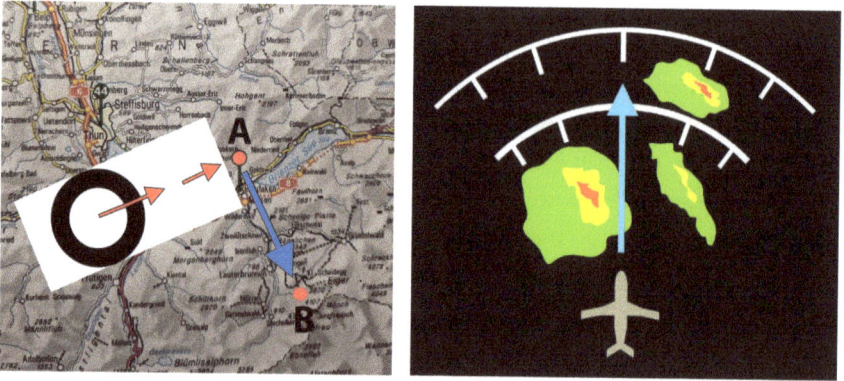

The Board materials also form a record of the communications and information provided to the Board. In most jurisdictions, the Board materials and the minutes of the Board meetings are required to be preserved as they form a record of the Board's deliberations and decision-making.

1.3.3.3. What are appropriate materials for the Board ?

Individual Board meetings through the year may have a specific focus. For example a meeting during the first quarter may focus on reviewing and finalizing accounts from the last year and performance appraisal matters. A meeting during the fourth quarter may focus on budgeting for the following year, including capital expenditure plans. Thus, Board materials for individual Board meetings will be a combination of information that is relevant for every Board meeting as well as information that is relevant for the focus of the specific Board meeting.

Information for each Board meeting

In light of the Board's responsibility to ensure compliance with regulatory and legal requirements, it is good practice for Boards to review and affirm continued adherence to regulatory and legal requirements or report noncompliance at each Board meeting. Once noncompliance is identified, the management will be required to provide further information in subsequent meetings on how it has been or is being addressed until back into compliance. Similarly, in each Board meeting it is good practice to confirm the absence of any health and safety issue arising between Board meetings or report any incidents and how they were dealt with.

It is customary that at each Board meeting, management will provide updates on financial and operational KPIs as agreed between the Board and management. Such updates will also need to include a narrative on financial and operational KPIs according to a template agreed between the Board and management. In addition, a comparison of actual performance along different metrics with the budget or plan and any revisions recommended to the plans and reasons for revisions need to be included in the Board materials. At each Board meeting the Directors should be provided with an update on operations and a market and competition summary.

Finally, in case there are any internal audit findings, the Board needs to be provided with updates on the responses from the audited managers or departments and the implementation of actions in response to such findings.

For start-ups, at each Board meeting management should discuss initiatives that may bring forward the cashflow break-even and progress ongoing fund-raising initiatives.

Information for Board meeting focused on accounts and CEO appraisal

The Board is responsible for the release of a publicly listed company's financial statements in line with listing requirements; or where the company is privately-held, for the submission of the company's accounts in accordance with the relevant regulatory requirements. Irrespective of its ownership status, the Board is also responsible for the company's submissions to the relevant tax authorities. Clearly these matters deserve thorough and timely discussion at the Board level prior to any communications in the form of statements, reports or submissions to third parties which create legal responsibilities and liabilities for the company and its Directors. The company's draft financial statements deserve centre stage in Board meetings that are focussed on the company's accounts and by extension the appraisal of the CEO's performance. Of course in addition to the financial statements, the executive management will need to provide commentary on these statements, specifically addressing items such as

- Sales growth, distinguishing between price and volume increases, as well as benchmarking for market growth to allow the Board to gauge any changes to the company's market share and competitive position
- Profitability at different levels, including gross margin, operating profit, earnings before interest, taxes, depreciation, and amortization (EBITDA), net income
- Cashflows including operating, investment and financing
- Leverage, with breakdowns of short-term and long-term borrowings as well as any off-balance-sheet items, debt service coverage and any covenant related issues
- Tax compliance and planning

Beyond establishing the actual performance, materials submitted to the Board by the executive management will need to provide comparisons between actual financial and operational performance relative to plan and budget. This can inform Board discussion and assessment of how well the executive management is delivering in terms of performance and adhering to agreed plans in terms of actions or establish the degree of deviations in actions and variances in performance and allow discussion of the drivers for such deviations and variances. Such discussion would have three objectives:

a. Establish in-line, out or under performance in a transparent and clear way
b. Allow the Board to consider appropriate reward or other action in relation to the executive management in light of their performance
c. Serve as confirmation that strategy is being implemented without need for corrective action or conversely serve as early warning of need to reconsider the company's strategy, priorities and plans.

Information for Board meeting focused on Risk Management and Human Resources Management

At least once a year, it is good practice for a Board to proactively focus its attention to Risk Management. Every business faces risks of many different types:

➤ risks to its mobile assets such as theft and accidents
➤ risks to its personnel including to their health and safety
➤ risks to its installations and equipment such as fire and flooding

It is one of the fundamental responsibilities of a Board to ensure that the company deals with such risks in an appropriate manner. In order to be in a position to do that, it is imperative that the executive management prepares and presents to the Board a comprehensive map of the risks the company is facing, identifying to the degree possible the likelihood and impact of each risk. Such a map can then be used to examine what risk mitigation measures can be taken. It is one of the most important responsibilities of a Board to ensure that the executive management has mapped out risks comprehensively **and** identified and recommended to the Board appropriate ways to deal with such risks. As the ultimate line of the company's Risk Management defence, the Board must respond to the management's recommendations with its decisions and direction. Such decisions and directions should be based on appropriate cost vs. benefit analyses and could be further informed by industry and competitor practice as well as the potential impact on the company's competitive position. However, as has already been established with the example of Johnson & Johnson removing all Tylenol tablets from the shelves, the values of the company can never be compromised and in some cases, particularly when it concerns customers' and employees' safety and well-being, there should be no tolerance for even the slightest chance of mishap. Intangibles like customer trust must also find their way into the Board's cost vs. benefit calculus.

Human resources is another area that deserves to be the focus of a Board meeting at least once a year. Beyond the obvious setting of budgets and compensation levels, including incentives, such a Board meeting can examine recruitment and training priorities as well as succession planning at senior levels. Moreover, development plans can be considered for senior and midlevel managers so that the company continues to expand and strengthen its pool of managerial talent. In all of these areas, the Board has a responsibility to make sure that management is proactive and does indeed have a human resources development plan that will maintain and strengthen the human capital of the company.

Information for Board meeting focused on markets, competition and strategy

Given the Board's responsibility for setting a company's strategy, it is imperative that the Board periodically focuses its discussions on markets, competition and strategy. The frequency of such Board discussions focused on strategy depends at least in part on the stage of the company's evolution as well as the industry in which it is competing. A company dominating a mature industry may not have need to discuss strategy as frequently as a start-up in a dynamic and changing market segment. However, the raw materials and tools for the discussion will be similar and will include:

a. Identification and assessment of market trends utilizing tools like political, economic, social, technological, environmental and legal (PESTEL) analysis
b. Profiling and benchmarking of competitors, including existing competitors' market positioning as well as new entrants
c. Analysis of the company's strengths, weaknesses, opportunities and threats (SWOT)

Some of the tools can interact with each other, as typically SWOT and PESTEL can do as illustrated below.

Figure 1.3.3.3.a. SWOT and PESTEL Analytical tools and their interrelationship

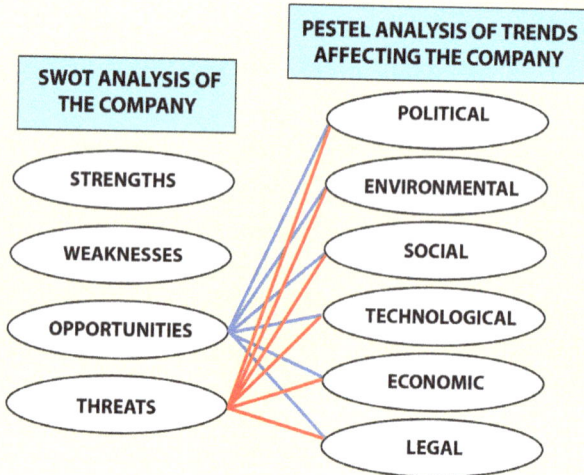

Fundamentally, the materials and tools are intended to allow the Board and management to discuss and consider different strategic options. Beyond analysing the advantages and disadvantages of each option, a Board must consider and address the resources required for the pursuit of each option and contrast it to the resources available or within reach. Prioritization of strategic options and allocation of resources can then follow. Thus, management teams must always bear this in mind when providing materials to their Board for a discussion and a decision on strategy. Beyond the narrative and recommendation on strategy and targets, a management team needs to also provide the observable facts and the analyses that underpins, in as solid a way as possible, their recommendations. Not surprisingly, the stage of evolution of a company influences the emphasis of the materials. For example, Boards of start-ups, need to be adept at securing adequate funding runways for their management teams to have time to execute. Consequently, management teams in such start-ups must be clear in their requests for capital, in terms of timing, amount and prospective use of requested capital. On the other hand, Boards of mature businesses, without many opportunities to deploy surplus capital profitably, must be particularly vigilant against trophy acquisitions and other similar "opportunities" championed as "strategic options" by empire-building CEOs and their teams.

Information for Board meeting focused on budgets

It is customary for most businesses to set annual budgets. So, at least one Board meeting a year has a focus on budgetary matters. Materials for Board discussions on budgets should include:

    a. Key financial targets and ratios including amongst others in respect of
- Sales growth
- Profitability at different levels (gross margin, operating profit, ebitda, net income)
- Cashflow and liquidity
- Leverage

    b. Key operational targets and ratios relevant to the industry including amongst others in respect of
- Capacity utilization
- Raw materials utilization

- Performance of production lines
- Warehouse/Distribution wastage

c. Procurement of raw materials – sources and pricing

d. Capital expenditures
- Maintenance capital expenditure (CapEx)
- Regulatory CapEx
- Growth related CapEx

e. Product mix targets

f. Market mix targets

g. Pricing targets

Financial performance commentary from the management to the Board

Commentary informs the Board as it explains the data presented to the Board. Thus, commentary needs to address variances, trends and events and not only offer explanations but also where appropriately proposals and recommendations for action.

In respect of Actual vs. Budget performance variances, management needs to provide information and explanations as to the drivers of the variances and break down how much of such variances are volume vs. price variances. For example, a significant positive variance in volume accompanied by no variance or even marginally negative variance in price signifying sales growth without significant erosion in profit margins, could be more welcome than an even greater positive variance in volume accompanied by a significant negative price variance indicating the growth was achieved at significantly lower than planned profit margins. As illustrated in the table below, a positive sales variance without an analysis of the price and volume variance that drive it, can mask eroding margins.

Figure 1.3.3.3.b. Price and Volume Variance analysis example

Price and Volume Variance Analysis - Example

COMPANY METRICS	BUDGET	SALES EXCEEDING BUDGET WITH NO SIGNIFICANT IMPACT ON MARGINS			SALES EXCEEDING BUDGET AT THE COST OF MARGINS	
		ACTUAL	VARIANCE		ACTUAL	VARIANCE
Sales price per unit	$ 20.00	$ 19.00	-5.0%		$ 15.00	-25.0%
Sales volume (units)	100,000	115,000	15.0%		150,000	50.0%
SALES	$ 2,000,000	$ 2,185,000	9.3%		$ 2,250,000	12.5%
Cost of Goods sold per unit	$ 14.00	$ 13.50	-3.6%		$ 13.00	-7.1%
Cost of Goods sold	$ 1,400,000	$ 1,552,500	10.9%		$ 1,950,000	39.3%
Gross Margin per unit	$ 6.00	$ 5.50	-8.3%		$ 2.00	-66.7%
Gross Margin % per unit	30%	29%	-3.3%		13.3%	-55.7%
Gross Margin	$ 600,000	$ 632,500	5.4%		$ 300,000	-50.0%

Of course, in addition to examining the breakdown between price and volume, management needs to place the company's performance in the context of market conditions. So, if market prices were significantly lower than budgeted, management would have had to risk losing market share if it did not also lower the pricing on the company's products. In such circumstances, the price and variance analysis needs to go one step further and place these variances in the context of market conditions in order to establish whether the company's performance is falling behind market competitors or not. Or as illustrated in the example below, consider a market which has remained stable in terms of volume and prices but in which the company managed to gain share without sacrificing margins or, conversely, gained share through heavy price discounting. The sales variance on its own could be positive in both scenarios but the true picture in terms of price, volume and profit margin variance would be very different in each. It would be reasonable for any Board to expect that the management would provide sufficiently detailed analyses to allow the true picture to emerge and discussed at the Board meeting.

Figure 1.3.3.3.c. Price and Volume Variance analysis including market conditions

Price and Volume Variance Analysis Example with market conditions taken into account					

		MARKET VOLUMES AND PRICE STABLE		MARKET VOLUMES AND PRICE STABLE	
MARKET OVERALL	BUDGET	ACTUAL	VARIANCE	ACTUAL	VARIANCE
Average market sales price per unit	$ 20.00	$ 19.75	-1.3%	$ 19.75	-1.3%
Total Market Volume (units)	500,000	510,000	2.0%	510,000	2.0%
Total Market Sales	$ 10,000,000.00	$ 10,072,500.00	0.7%	$10,072,500.00	0.7%
		COMPANY IS GAINING SHARE WITH MILD PRICE DISCOUNTING		COMPANY IS BUYING MARKET SHARE WITH HEAVY PRICE DISCOUNTING AT COST TO MARGIN	
COMPANY METRICS	BUDGET	ACTUAL	VARIANCE	ACTUAL	VARIANCE
Sales price per unit	$ 20.00	$ 19.00	-5.0%	$ 15.00	-25.0%
Sales volume (units)	100,000	114,500	14.5%	145,000	45.0%
SALES	$ 2,000,000.00	$ 2,175,500.00	8.8%	$ 2,175,000.00	8.8%
Cost of Goods sold per unit	$ 14.00	$ 13.50	-3.6%	$ 13.00	-7.1%
Cost of Goods sold	$ 1,400,000.00	$ 1,545,750.00	10.4%	$ 1,885,000.00	34.6%
Gross Margin per unit	$ 6.00	$ 5.50	-8.3%	$ 2.00	-66.7%
Gross Margin % per unit	30.0%	28.9%	-3.5%	13.3%	-55.7%
Gross Margin	$ 600,000.00	$ 629,750.00	5.0%	$ 290,000.00	-51.7%
Company volume market share		20.0%	22.5%	12.3%	28.4%	42.0%
Company sales market share		20.0%	21.6%	8.0%	21.6%	8.0%

In case there are persistent trends that are becoming evident which are affecting performance, management needs to not only acknowledge them and whether performance is getting better or worse as a result, but also offer at least some informed opinion as to the factors, both external and internal, that may be driving or influencing such trends. Based on their diagnosis, management would be expected to also recommend actions to maintain favourable trends or actions to arrest unfavourable trends. As trends do not persist forever, management also needs to be ready to discuss expected departures from trends and factors which can cause such changes.

Individual events may also affect performance and where that is the case management needs to offer informed opinion as to whether such an event is a one-time event or not and assess the external and internal factors that may be driving or influencing such events.

Any financial commentary by management also needs to proactively address critical levels of performance that may be requiring attention or action. By identifying areas in need of improvement in performance or condition such as leverage that is too high, liquidity that is getting too stretched, working capital financing that is too expensive, receivables that are rising or are too high, inventory turns that are slowing or too low, etc.), management can seek and secure timely Board support for initiatives and resources that could help achieve appropriate improvements.

Finally, since very few companies enjoy monopoly conditions, financial performance commentary also needs to benchmark the company's financial performance with the financial performance of its key competitors so that management and Board can jointly examine the company's performance in relative terms and whether the company's position is getting stronger or weaker.

Operational performance commentary from the management to the Board

Commentary for operational performance can follow a similar template as for financial performance commentary and address variances, trends and events.

Materials for the Board regarding procurement budgeting

Procurement budgeting should be an opportunity for a supplier review and benchmarking. Therefore, for each supplier, management needs to provide the Board with information on how much of the company's needs they supply, under what pricing and terms of supply, the nature and length of the relationship and whether the supplier is also supplying to the company's competitors. In addition, for each supplier there should be an assessment by management of the company's importance to the supplier and whether there is room for better pricing or terms. Similarly, for potential new suppliers, management needs to provide the Board with information on how much of the company's needs they could supply, under what pricing and terms and how important the company could become to the supplier. In addition, management needs to identify and quantify any switching costs and project what type of relationship may be feasible with the prospective new supplier, especially if they are also supplying to the competition. Such disciplined analysis and benchmarking of procurement options, can often help add value even without switching.

Materials for the Board for benchmarking product and market mix relative to market trends and potential

Board discussions on budgets, strategy and performance will often take in the company's product and market mix performance and targets. Such discussions will be better informed and lead to better decision-making if management provides the Board with relevant market information as well as the company's own performance. Thus for product mix benchmarking, management needs to provide information on both growth and pricing trends since the aim would be to maintain or increase market share and maintain or increase margins. Beyond market growth and pricing trends, management also needs to be vigilant and inform the Board of any consolidation trends. Once again the objective is to maintain or increase the company's position and pricing power with clients and suppliers.

For market mix benchmarking, management needs to provide the Board with information on market segments size and potential with the aim being to be present in large markets and in markets with strong or accelerating growth potential. Similar to product mix, for market mix management will need to address growth, pricing and consolidation trends. Normally both management and Board would be aiming to be present in large markets and markets with strong or accelerating growth potential and to maintain or increase margins. Management also needs to examine if concentration conditions and consolidation trends may present an opportunity for the company to become a dominant player with market power, either through organic growth or through merger and acquisition activity.

Materials for the Board regarding pricing targets within a competitive environment

Whilst individual prices for individual products or services may not be a matter for the Board, the way in which management sets pricing targets is definitely something over which the Board should exercise oversight of management. In this context, management needs to explain to the Board the factors it considers in setting prices for the company's products or services. Since most companies face competition for their goods and services, pricing targets cannot be considered outside the context of the relevant competitive environment and indeed the first factor to be considered, including at Board level, is the competitive pricing landscape. And how management gauges the company's target customers' perception of the company price proposition, and what is that perception, are both very much of interest to the company's Board. Pricing trends and the drivers of such trends are another important factor that needs to be taken into account. But as price is not the only dimension on which companies compete, Board materials should also examine what other dimensions are relevant in customers' purchasing decisions and establish the relative importance of pricing within a specific product or market category. For example, reliability, aesthetics or prestige are dimensions that can trump pricing considerations for car buyers in certain car market segments. Competitors' pricing stance is also important to consider as it can help establish where the company's own pricing places it in the aggressive lead vs passive follower spectrum.

Information for Board meeting focused on capital expenditure planning

Periodically a Board will be asked to approve capital expenditures. Discussion on capital expenditures may arise

- a. in order to remain compliant with regulatory requirements (Regulatory CapEx) or
- b. in the context of maintaining existing capacities and capabilities (Maintenance CapEx) or
- c. as part of strategic options under consideration for growing the business (Growth CapEx).

These three different types of capital expenditure are driven by different considerations and therefore it is incumbent for any management presenting CapEx proposals to its Board to correctly characterise the nature of the proposed CapEx because this will also determine the information they will need to provide to the Board in support of their proposal.

Regulatory CapEx, as mentioned already, is driven by a need to maintain or achieve compliance with a regulatory requirement. Such a requirement may be linked to the environment or health and safety. Management needs to explain how a new or changing requirement is creating a potential compliance gap that needs attention and action. Board materials should also include an assessment of the risks and costs of noncompliance, such as penalties, reputation risks, effects on the labour-force, effects on clients and other stakeholders. Management should identify the CapEx that would be needed to ensure compliance as well as any training that may be needed and a reasonable timetable to reach compliance. In short, Board materials should identify what needs to be done, by whom, at what cost and by when.

Maintenance CapEx is obviously linked to maintaining capacities and capabilities. Therefore when requesting Board approval for maintenance CapEx, management needs first to explain what level of capacity is appropriate to maintain. Whilst depreciation is in some industries considered a good proxy for maintenance CapEx, budgeting for maintenance CapEx should not be simply guided by historical costs and requirements. In a fashion similar to regulatory CapEx, management should also discuss the risks arising in the absence of maintenance CapEx. In cases where the company has relevant internal capabilities, management should also present to the Board a comparison between CapEx done in-house vs. outsourced so that the most efficient and cost-effective option can be selected.

Growth CapEx is part and parcel of strategic growth and as such it can be driven by a number of different opportunities, like the launch of a new product, the introduction of a new production line to meet expanding sales or addressing a production bottleneck. For each type of opportunity, management needs to provide the cost benefit analysis, including any opportunity costs that the specific growth CapEx is intended to nullify such as CapEx to remove a bottleneck and mitigate loss of production and revenues. Management also needs to offer the Board their clear assessment of the company's internal capacity to implement the proposed Growth CapEx compared with an externally project managed implementation process. Procurement and implementation costs and timing of start and delivery of Growth CapEx are also important parameters to be discussed with the Board. Of course Board materials need to include analysis and benchmarking of different options of implementing growth related CapEx, so that the right option can be selected. Overall, materials for a Board discussion of growth CapEx should include answers to the why, what, who, how, how much and by when.

Common to all three types of CapEx is that there will usually be more than one potential solution with each possible solution having its own advantages and disadvantages. Therefore, management needs to compare and contrast different options in terms of:

- Technical feasibility and potential technical advantages and disadvantages
- Implications and any requirements placed on human resources
- Financial attractiveness (return on investment, payback period, net present value, internal rate of return)
- Financing options and possibilities

All the above should drive clear management recommendations on CapEx and Board decision-making.

1.3.4. Board of Directors – Balanced Board of Directors

What makes a Board of Directors balanced?

As already discussed, a Board of Directors has specific decision-making powers and is the main oversight body of a company that can hold management to account. A balanced Board has certain characteristics that are clear and obvious to all stakeholders. They are:

a. Uncompromisingly ethical and acting with integrity
b. Sufficiently independent from management
c. Mindful of all shareholders' and stakeholders' interests
d. Sufficiently experienced in areas that are critical to the success of the business such as markets, products and functions
e. Sufficiently inclusive and diverse **in ways that matter to the success of the business**, including gender, age and race
f. Compatible personalities, achieving reasonable working functionality without succumbing to group think

So, there are six important dimensions to aim for in order to have a balanced Board of Directors

Figure 1.3.4.a. Six critical dimensions for a balanced Board of Directors

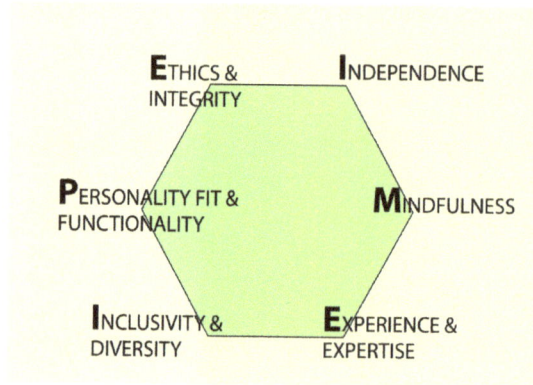

An easy acronym for these is **EIMEIP**. Another way to look at these six dimensions is as three interrelated pairs:

✓ Independence can also safeguard integrity and ethics – it is much more likely to have a Board which acts with Integrity and in an Ethical manner if its members are truly independent from senior management

✓ Mindfulness can also underpin functionality and personal fit – it is much more likely the Board will avoid dysfunctionality if its members are truly mindful of where their duty of care lies

✓ Diversity and inclusivity also ensures broader and more relevant Experience and Expertise – it is much more likely the Board will not be blinkered and succumb to group think

Figure 1.3.4.b. Interrelationship of critical dimensions for a Board of Directors

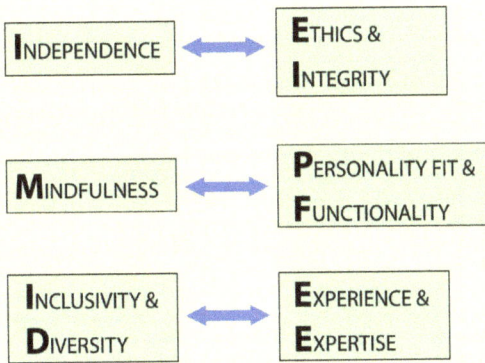

Why does it matter? How does it help to have a balanced Board of Directors?

In simple terms, a balanced Board of Directors has a better chance of fulfilling its mandate since it can:

a. Become a liability to the business and its prospects if it acts unethically or without integrity
b. More easily hold management to account if it is sufficiently independent from management
c. More easily ensure the company's direction is consistent with the shareholders' and stakeholders' interests, if its members are mindful of these interests
d. Interact more efficiently and effectively with management plus support and contribute management effort's where appropriate if they have relevant experience
e. Anticipate and appreciate more deeply and clearly opportunities, risks and challenges with the benefit of diverse, inclusive and by extension wider perspectives
f. Maintain better efficiency, effectiveness and responsiveness if it avoids group think and dysfunctionality

How do we ensure our Board of Directors is balanced?

The individual components of EIMEIP are often assessed by reference to the credentials of individual Board members. Compliance with some dimensions is more readily achievable and observable than others. A well-functioning Board under the leadership of an effective Chairman will usually have a Nominations Committee that will monitor and review the Board's own composition and periodically make relevant recommendations. External advisors can sometimes play a role in achieving a balanced Board of Directors.

It is sometimes obvious that a Board is not balanced or sufficiently diverse. Consider a computer video gaming company or a cosmetics company with a Board made up exclusively of white men who are all over 70 years of age. Such a Board would fail in diversity in terms of age, race and gender in both cases.

But sometimes even with age, race and gender boxes ticked off, Boards can still be insufficiently diverse. Consider a company with international operations with a Board made up of executives and non-executives who are all native of the country where the company is headquartered and have all attended the same or similar schools and universities and have similar professional qualifications. In such a Board, if the formative experiences and influences of the Board members are essentially the same, even if there is diversity of race, gender and age, who will offer a perspective that is somewhat different from the rest of the Board?

Diversity is a much more nuanced requirement than simply a box ticking exercise and Chairmen and Nominations Committees forget that at their peril.

Similarly, consider a Board that is made up of strong and abrasive personalities. Even if they meet all the other criteria, they are likely to be fundamentally incompatible and render their Board dysfunctional if they all rub each other the wrong way all the time. Thus, both a Chairman and a Nominating Committee need to consider not only the individual qualities of individual directors but also the sum of all the directors and their likely interactions when asked to function as a collective body.

1.3.5. Risk Management

1.3.5.1. What is Risk?

Risk is a situation involving danger and uncertain outcomes. It is an uncertain event or condition that if it occurs, has an effect on at least one objective or actor. It can also be defined as the probability or threat of quantifiable damage, injury, liability, loss or any other negative occurrence that is caused by external or internal vulnerabilities, and that may be avoided through pre-emptive action. In Finance, risk is often defined as the probability that an actual return on an investment or activity will be lower than the expected return.

Every business faces risks and risks affect every aspect of business. As illustrated in the diagram below, they can be grouped in four categories depending on their nature.

Figure 1.3.5.1.a. Categories of business risks

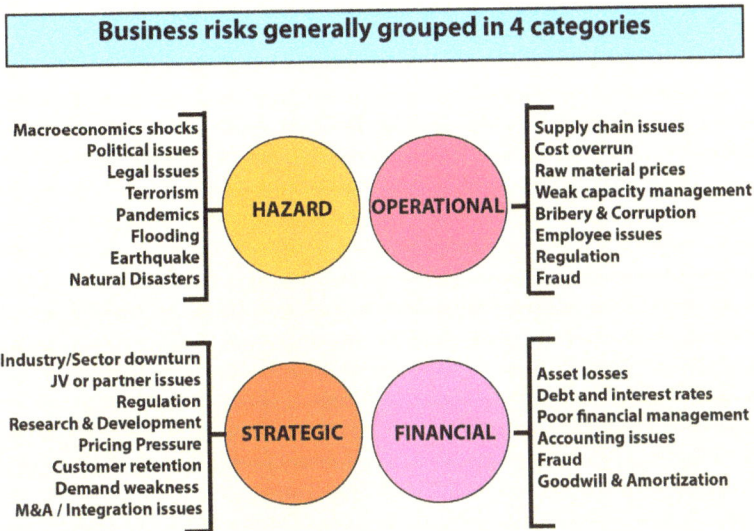

Business risks generally grouped in 4 categories

Macroeconomics shocks
Political issues
Legal Issues
Terrorism
Pandemics
Flooding
Earthquake
Natural Disasters

HAZARD

OPERATIONAL

Supply chain issues
Cost overrun
Raw material prices
Weak capacity management
Bribery & Corruption
Employee issues
Regulation
Fraud

Industry/Sector downturn
JV or partner issues
Regulation
Research & Development
Pricing Pressure
Customer retention
Demand weakness
M&A / Integration issues

STRATEGIC

FINANCIAL

Asset losses
Debt and interest rates
Poor financial management
Accounting issues
Fraud
Goodwill & Amortization

1.3.5.2. What is Risk Management ?

Risk Management is the discipline (i.e. practices, policies and procedures) and function (i.e. people and their internal and external interactions) that a business introduces in order to manage risks and safeguard against distress and failure. Depending on the nature of the business, Risk Management is practiced at different levels in the business, including in some cases at the Board level through specialist Risk Committees (for example in banks or insurance companies).

As illustrated in the diagram below, Risk Management can be thought of as a continuous process whereby at different levels in the business, there is identification of risks, which leads to analysis and assessment of risks so that their likelihood and impact or consequences can be gauged. This assessment informs planning and implementation of appropriate policies. These can include accepting the risk and in effect self-insuring, or transferring the risk via the insurance market. In some circumstances, if the risk is deemed potentially too catastrophic to bear and impossible to transfer, risk will need to be avoided via changing policies or products or even discontinuing activities. The loop closes via active monitoring, measuring and reporting the effectiveness of the risk mitigation.

Figure 1.3.5.2.a. Risk Management as a process

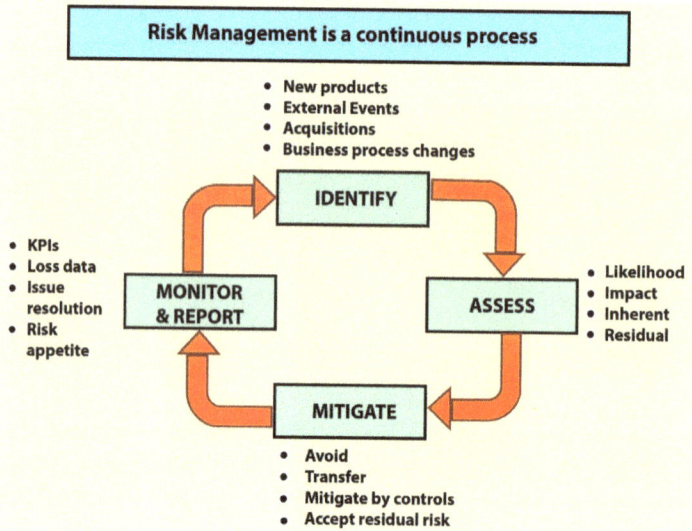

Risk Management involves management decision-making about individual risks and about classes of risks. Some risks can be accepted and in effect the business is self-insuring such risks. These risks tend to be low impact and low probability type risks. Other risks, that can have much greater impact but are still low probability can usually be transferred to third parties that provide insurance for these risks. Examples of such risks can be flooding or fire risks. Risks that are quite likely but of low impact individually, are best dealt with via risk mitigation measures. For example shoplifting is a major risk for retailers and supermarkets which is usually addressed via technological risk mitigation measures and some old fashioned personnel muscle. The most troublesome risks are catastrophe type risks for which cover is usually not available through the insurance market. Such risks are best avoided and indeed prudent Risk Management may mean redesigning business activities or even abandoning them to ensure the business is insulated from the risk. Sometimes it is possible to contract activities which carry such risk to third parties who are prepared to take on such risks. For example, oil companies avoid the risk of oil pollution in the maritime transportation of their cargoes, by procuring the services of independent tanker shipping companies.

Figure 1.3.5.2.b. Management options arising from Risk Management

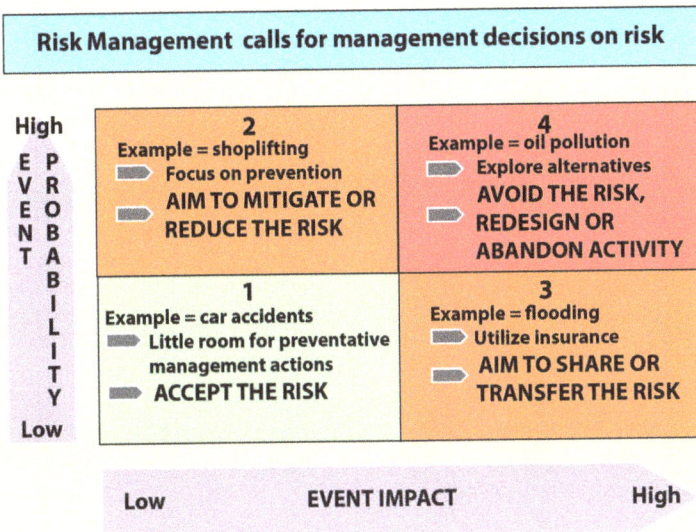

Risk Management calls for management decisions on risk

	2	4
High	Example = shoplifting	Example = oil pollution
EVENT PROBABILITY	➡ Focus on prevention	➡ Explore alternatives
	➡ AIM TO MITIGATE OR REDUCE THE RISK	➡ AVOID THE RISK, REDESIGN OR ABANDON ACTIVITY
	1	3
	Example = car accidents	Example = flooding
	➡ Little room for preventative management actions	➡ Utilize insurance
Low	➡ ACCEPT THE RISK	➡ AIM TO SHARE OR TRANSFER THE RISK

Low   EVENT IMPACT   High

For the risks that a company decides it can accept and not transfer or for which there is no escape from and yet still no cover, there is the optional tool of setting up the company's own insurance company. Such companies are known as "captives" since their only function is to serve the insurance needs of its owners. They are usually operated from jurisdictions that have friendly regulatory requirements for captive insurance companies (for example Bermuda, Channel Islands, Luxembourg). They charge premiums to their parent or sister subsidiaries and they can cede some part of the risk they take on by reinsuring some of their exposure with third party reinsurers. They generate investment income on the premiums they collect and build up reserves in the same way as third-party insurance companies. Crucially, the reserves they accumulate over time, can be used for the benefit of the parent rather than fund dividends and profits for the shareholders of third-party insurers. Thus, captives can, over time, become a source of balance sheet resilience for their parents whilst continuing to cover risks at a cost which management considers competitive and good value relative to the third-party insurance market.

1.3.5.3. Why does Risk Management matter?

Risk is rarely eliminated completely in business and no business can generate returns without taking on some measure of risk. But equally many a business has failed due to taking on too much risk. Where can a business draw the line and balance risk and reward? That is the question that Risk Management, as a discipline and as a function, is intended to help address. Therefore, in the absence of Risk Management, a business may be taking on too much risk without even knowing it. There is therefore a clear benefit from incorporating Risk Management in the overall Corporate Governance of a company. It helps reduce the risk of distress or failure. And on the flipside, it allows companies to at least calculate risks and rewards when faced with major decisions and take appropriate decisions in a methodical and transparent way.

Figure 1.3.5.3.a. Costs/Benefits of Risk Management

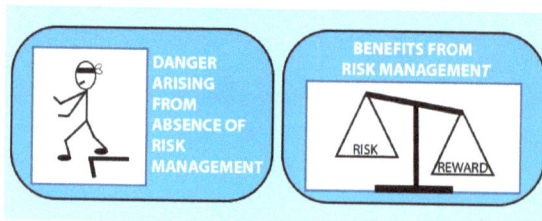

1.3.5.4. How do you introduce Risk Management?

The oversight body of a company, (usually the Board of Directors) will often have a Risk Committee that will be concerned with the risks taken on by the business and will have regular interaction with the senior managers of the business tasked with Risk Management. Depending on the nature and extend of risks inherent in the business activities of the company, Risk Management may be handled by a dedicated team of executives with their leader either reporting to or being part of the senior executive team of the company for example a Chief Risk Officer, or the CFO.

Figure 1.3.5.4.a. Risk Management Organizational structure

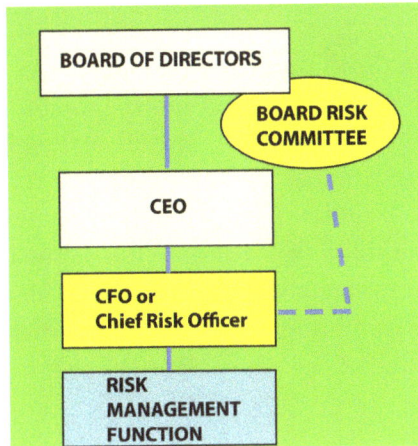

1.3.5.5. The Risk Management Matrix tool

What is the Risk Management Matrix tool?

The Risk Management Matrix tool, as the name implies and as illustrated in the diagram is a tool that allows the mapping of risks along a two-dimensional grid with the probability of occurrence of a risk being one of the dimensions and the severity of impact from the occurrence of a risk being the other dimension. By representing each risk on the grid through two dimensional coordinates based on the assessment of each risk's probability and impact, the matrix allows comparison of multiple risks and provides a means by which to compare and contrast risks and consider appropriate action.

As can be seen from the illustration of the tool in the diagram below, the level of granularity can be chosen to suit the needs of a particular business. It can be as simple as a high – low distinction leading to a matrix with four quadrants as in the left-hand matrix in the diagram below. It can be made more granular by choosing how many steps to introduce between the two ends of the spectrum. In the right-hand matrix diagram example below, the matrix allows distinguishing between low, medium and high probability and impact. So, the matrix yields nine spaces distinct spaces based on the 3 x 3 combinations of probability and impact pairs.

Figure 1.3.5.5.a. Risk Management Matrix Tool

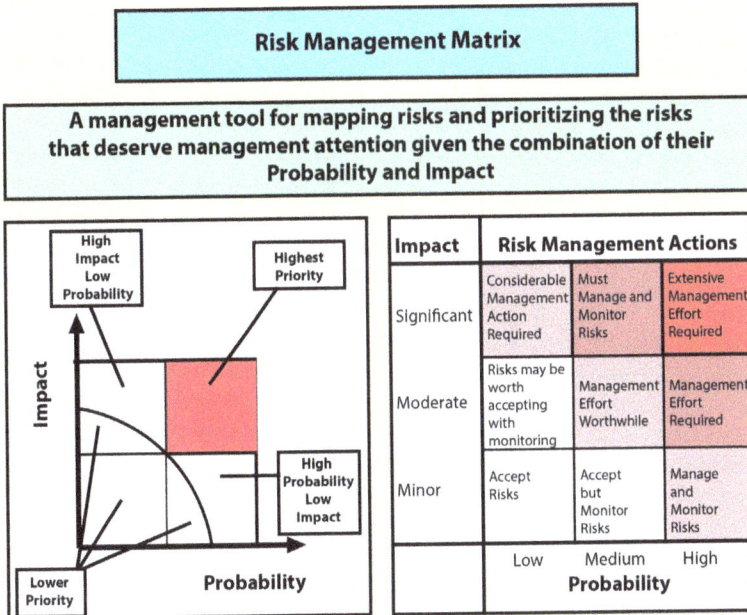

Risk Management Matrix

A management tool for mapping risks and prioritizing the risks that deserve management attention given the combination of their Probability and Impact

Impact	Risk Management Actions		
	Low	**Medium**	**High**
Significant	Considerable Management Action Required	Must Manage and Monitor Risks	Extensive Management Effort Required
Moderate	Risks may be worth accepting with monitoring	Management Effort Worthwhile	Management Effort Required
Minor	Accept Risks	Accept but Monitor Risks	Manage and Monitor Risks
	Low	Medium	High
		Probability	

High Impact Low Probability

Highest Priority

High Probability Low Impact

Lower Priority

Impact

Probability

How to construct and use a Risk Management Matrix

The first step in constructing a Risk Management Matrix, is to determine the desired level of granularity by reference to the number and nature of the risks to be covered. Risks for this purpose can be defined used the CASE tool by answering the following questions:

- **C**onsequence – what is the impact of this risk?
- **A**sset – what assets are at risk?
- **S**ource – what are the hazards or threat actors behind this risk?
- **E**vent – what particular type of incident is being considered?

In addition, for both the impact dimension and the probability dimension, the spectrum from low to high needs to be divided in as many steps as is desirable. In relation to the impact ratings, the steps can be designed by quantifying such impact. In relation to the probability ratings, the steps can be designed through the use of historical experience. The diagram below provides examples of ratings for the impact and probability dimensions, with five steps in each dimension.

Figure 1.3.5.5.b. Constructing a Risk Management Matrix

Impact / Consequences Ratings - Illustrative example

Rating	Property	Economic
Insignificant	Minor damage or vandalism	1% of project or annual budget
Negligible	Minor damage or loss of < 5% of total assets	2-5% of project or annual budget
Moderate	Damage or loss of < 20% of total assets	5-10% of project or annual budget
Extensive	Extensive damage or loss of < 50% of total assets	> 10% of project or annual budget
Significant	Destruction or complete loss of > 50% of total assets	> 30% of project or annual budget

Probability Ratings - Illustrative example

Rating	Chance	Frequency	Probability
Almost Certain	Occur in most circumstances	Has occured 9 or 10 times in past 10 years or in this organization	> 95%
Likely	Will probably occur in most circumstances	Has occured more than 7 times in past 10 years in this organization or similar organizations or circumstances, such that it is likely it wil happen again in the next few years	> 65%
Possible	Might occur at some time	Has occured in this organization 3 times in past 10 years or occurs regularly in similar organizations or has reasonable likelihood of occuring in the next few years	> 35%
Unlikely	Could occur some time	Has occured 2 or 3 times in the past 10 years in this organization or similar organizations	35% <
Rare	May occur only in exceptional circumstances	Has occured or can be reasonably expected to occur only a few times in 100 years	5% <

The combination of consequence and likelihood descriptors creates a Risk Management Matrix and as already explained, mapping risks on the matrix helps identify priorities in need of management attention and decisions. In the example shown below the Risk Management Matrix has 25 distinct spaces based on the five steps along each dimension as described above.

Figure 1.3.5.5.c. Risk Management Matrix – output

5 x 5 Risk Management Matrix - Example

5	Significant	6	7	8	9	10
4	Extensive	5	6	7	8	9
3	Moderate	4	5	6	7	8
2	Negligible	3	4	5	6	7
1	Insignificant	2	3	4	5	6
		Rare	Unlikely	Possible	Likely	Almost Certain
		1	2	3	4	5

Benefits from using Risk Management Matrix

Using a Risk Management Matrix in dealing with risk offers a number of benefits:

- ✓ Provides consistency and granularity to risk prioritization
- ✓ Encourages and facilitates robust discussion
- ✓ Provides a point of focus when assessing risks
- ✓ Presents complex data concisely and in visually insightful fashion

Limitations of Risk Management Matrix

But Risk Management Matrices also have limitations:

- ➤ They can correctly and unambiguously compare only a small fraction of selected pairs of hazards and can assign identical ratings to quantitatively different risks

> ➤ They can mistakenly assign higher qualitative ratings to quantitatively smaller risks to the point where with risks that have negatively correlated frequencies and severities, they can lead to worse-than-random decisions
> ➤ They can result in suboptimal resource allocation as effective allocation of resources to risk treatments cannot be based on the categories provided by risk matrices
> ➤ The categorization of severity cannot be made objectively for uncertain consequences. Assessment of probability and impact and resulting risk ratings require a subjective interpretation and different users may obtain substantially different ratings of the same quantitative risks
> ➤ They do not include any assessment of timeframes affecting risks as they are a snapshot in time
> ➤ They can oversimplify the complexity or volatility of a risk as some risks are relatively static and others can change for better or worse very quickly

Limits of the limitations

Yet, there are also limits to the above-mentioned limitations, including:

- ✓ Prioritizing allocation of resources is not the role of the risk matrix
- ✓ Any risk assessment tool can assign identical ratings to quantitatively different risks
- ✓ No tool can consistently correctly and unambiguously compare more than a small fraction of hazards
- ✓ Risk matrices are designed to provide qualitative or semi-quantitative ordinal information (i.e. relative priority), not mathematically precise data
- ✓ If a risk is in the high attention category it requires attention and its relative position within the category (e.g. first vs. fourth) is not likely to be significant
- ✓ Inherent limitations of human decision-making under uncertainty processes of human risk perception mean subjective decision-making will always be part of the risk assessment process irrespective of the tool used
- ✓ Risk matrices are a tool which support risk informed decisions, not a tool for making decisions
- ✓ Risk matrices are a practical tool that is not meant to be used in isolation

On balance, as with any other tool, the Risk Management Matrix is as helpful and effective as its users allow it to be. It contributes to better outcomes when used carefully and without exaggerating its abilities and potential contribution or ignoring its limitations. Fundamentally it is a tool aimed at facilitating the exercise of management judgment and it is the way such judgment is indeed exercised that determines in the end the value of the Risk Management Matrix as a tool.

1.3.5.6. The Internal Risk Controls tool

What are Internal Risk Controls?

Each organization tries to reduce the risks it faces. By reducing risk for the business, the prospects of attaining the objectives of the business increases. The actions, decisions, policies and procedures that a business uses, on a repeated ongoing basis or in one-off applications, intended to reduce risk can be considered to be the Internal Risk Controls of the business. They are another tool in Risk Management.

Figure 1.3.5.6.a. Internal Risk Controls tool

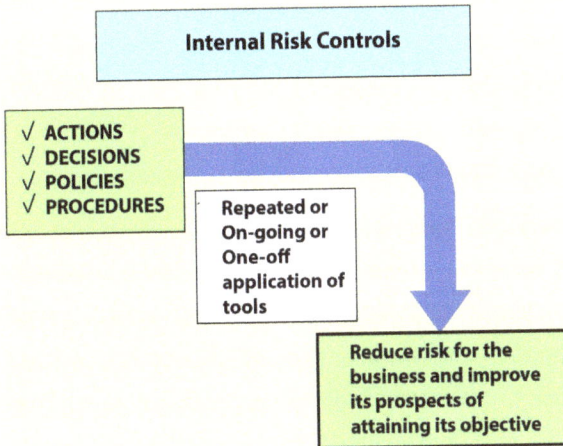

Why are Internal Risk Controls important?

Internal Risk Controls are an important part of Risk Management since they are intended to prevent risks from materializing or if they do materialize to minimize their impact on the business. Institutionalizing Internal Risk Controls is therefore an important part of Corporate Governance. Every decision-maker, indeed everyone in a business needs to be concerned with observing the Internal Risk Controls that are relevant to their activities and decision-making. Many of the simplest Internal Risk Controls, for example a company policy not to allow anyone into company premises without appropriate identification, or locking company cars when not in use even in company warehouses can be considered common sense. They are no less important for that. At their core, all Internal Risk Controls aim to achieve or contribute to:

- ✓ **C**ompliance with applicable laws and regulations
- ✓ **A**ccomplishment of the entity's mission
- ✓ **R**elevant and reliable financial reporting
- ✓ **E**ffective and efficient operations
- ✓ **S**afeguarding of assets

Combining the initial capitals we get **CARES**, and it is true that effective internal controls reduce cares and ineffective internal controls increase cares.

Risks arising from weak Internal Risk Controls

The risks that arise from weak or ineffective Internal Risk Controls can be quite serious with very serious consequences for the business:

- ➢ System breakdowns or catastrophes in the processes of the business or situations where absent or weak controls lead to excessive re-work to correct errors (for example on a production line) can lead to significant business interruption with knock-on effects on sales, cashflow, profitability, customer relations and market share
- ➢ Erroneous, inadequate or misleading information that is generated inside the business and used by management can lead to erroneous management decisions with distressing consequences
- ➢ Absence or weak internal controls can create conditions that may allow fraud, embezzlement and theft by management or employees or customers or vendors or the public at large

➤ Absent or weak internal controls may result in regulatory non-compliance and statutory sanctions and penalties for such non-compliance

➤ Absent or weak internal controls can affect the way expenses are incurred and recorded and the way sales are achieved and recognized and this can lead to excessive costs or deficient revenues

➤ Without internal controls or when controls are not properly observed, there can be loss, misuse or destruction of assets, including physical assets such as cash, inventory and equipment

Benefits of strong Internal Risk Controls

As is the case with poor Corporate Governance the negative consequences of which are much more noticeable and commented on, than the ways in which good Corporate Governance keeps a business from distress, the benefits from strong Internal Risk Controls working effectively are priorities that are often taken for granted including:

✓ Providing appropriate checks and balances
✓ Reducing and preventing errors in a cost-effective manner
✓ Ensuring priority issues and risks are identified and addressed
✓ Protecting employees and resources
✓ Having more efficient audits, resulting in shorter timelines, less testing and fewer demands on staff

Key Internal Control activities

It is clear from the preceding analysis of risks arising from weak Internal Risk Controls and the benefits accruing from strong ones, that it is highly desirable to aim for strong Internal Risk Controls. But how are such controls to be achieved? There are five key internal control activities which can enhance the prospects of achieving strong Internal Risk Controls. They are:

1. Separation of duties

It is both common sense and a fundamental key internal control to divide responsibilities between different employees so one individual doesn't control all aspects of a transaction, a decision or an activity. For example traders are not meant to be their own back-office. Such separation reduces the opportunity for an employee to commit and conceal errors, whether intentional or unintentional, or to perpetrate fraud. Most employees do not seek to take on more and more responsibility and are not averse to limitations placed on their responsibilities through separation of duties. They also know that separation of duties is protection for them too from unintentional mistakes. Employers should worry more when employees object to such separation of duties than when they accept it.

2. Documentation

Another fundamental Internal Risk Control activity is to keep records and document all elements that affect the business for future internal and possibly external reference, including:

- ✓ Critical decisions and significant events –typically those involving the use, commitment or transfer of resources
- ✓ Transactions – enabling each transaction to be traced from its inception to completion
- ✓ Policies and procedures – documents the fundamental principles and methods that employees rely on to do their jobs
- ✓ Controls – should be documented to be evidenced

3. Authorization and approvals

Many businesses processes require specific actions at specific times. It is an important Internal Risk Control to have clarity as to who is authorised to take what action and how approvals are sought and given for specific actions. Therefore an important internal risk activity is to require management to:

- ✓ Document and communicate to all relevant staff which activities require approval, and by whom. Such approvals may be tiered and also linked to the level of risk to the organization
- ✓ Ensure that transactions are approved and executed only by employees acting within the scope of their authority delegated to them by management (e.g. such delegated authority limits may include specific expenditure or investment limits)
- ✓ Ensure all employees with delegated authority limits do indeed understand the limits of their authority, how to avoid exceeding them and when and how to refer or escalate matters to more senior staff with greater delegated authority limits.

4. Security of Assets

The physical security of the assets of the business is another vital Internal Risk Control and management has a responsibility to:

- ✓ Secure and restrict access to equipment, cash, inventory, confidential information and the like to reduce the risk of loss or unauthorized use
- ✓ Perform periodic physical inventories to verify existence, quantities, location, condition and utilization
- ✓ Secure access to key IT resources and systems
- ✓ Base the level of security on the vulnerability of items being secured, the likelihood of loss, and the potential impact should a loss occur

5. Reconciliation and Review

Finally, an important internal control activity concerns the timely monitoring and review of activities inside the business so corrective action can be taken in a timely fashion if the need arises. This internal control activity involves:

- ✓ Examining transactions, information and events to verify accuracy, completeness, appropriateness and compliance
- ✓ Determining the level of review based on materiality, risk and overall importance to the organization's activities
- ✓ Ensuring frequency is adequate enough to detect and act upon questionable activities in a timely manner
- ✓ Conducting tiered level reviews

1.3.5.7. Board Involvement in Risk Management

Risk can never be completely eliminated from business activity and incorporating Risk Management into a company's Corporate Governance framework and culture, has clear benefits for the business. It follows that as a body responsible for ensuring that good Corporate Governance is practiced, a Board has an active role in ensuring Risk Management is indeed appropriately practiced. Thus even though it is the executive management of the business that primarily uses the tools mentioned (i.e. Risk Management Matrix and Internal Risk Controls), the Board has a clear and ongoing responsibility to ensure such tools are used with care and not abused or ignored.

1.3.6. Internal Audit Function

1.3.6.1. What is Agency Risk and Asymmetry of Information?

Managers are "agents" for the owners and are meant to serve the interests of the owners of the business as they manage the business. Placing managers in control of business activities creates an asymmetry of information between them and the owners of the business because managers have more information than owners. This asymmetry of information requires the owners to monitor managers effectively in order to ensure that managers are indeed appropriately serving the interests of the owners of the business because managers who are not also owners create "agency" risk and costs when they do not serve the owners' interests as they discharge their duties as managers.

Figure 1.3.6.1.a. The Principal vs Agent Conundrum in Governance terms

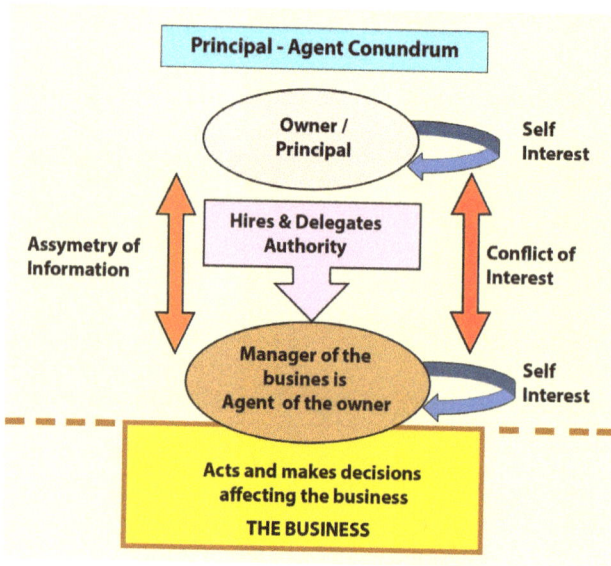

1.3.6.2. What is the Internal Audit Function?

Internal monitoring of management is an important function that minimizes the agency risks and costs we have examined above. This function is described as the Internal Audit Function (IAF) and in order to preserve its independence from management and ensure its objectivity and effectiveness, it is common practice for the IAF to report directly to the oversight body, very often the Board of Directors, which is elected by the owners or shareholders of the business and is tasked with keeping executive management accountable, and not to the executive management. The IAF is often likened to the "eyes and ears" of the Board of Directors.

Figure 1.3.6.2.a. IAF position in organizational structure

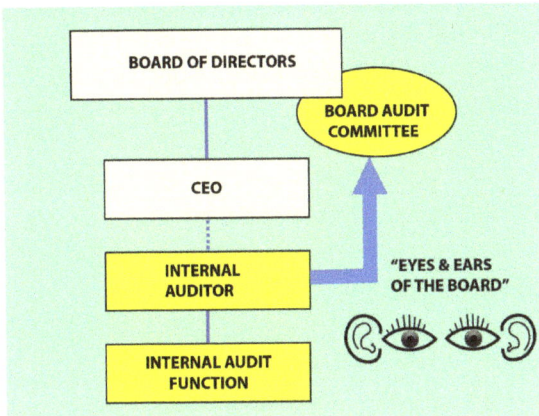

The IAF is a service function as it assists members of the organization, including management and the Board, in the effective discharge of their responsibilities by:

- ✓ Providing information, analysis and appraisals
- ✓ Making recommendations and giving advice
- ✓ Monitoring issues identified until and how they are resolved

IAF role and responsibilities

The IAF is established by the Board of Directors or the Board audit committee and the IAF's responsibilities are defined by the Board or Board Audit Committee as part of their oversight role. The scope of IAF encompasses, but is not limited to:

- ✓ Examination and evaluation of the adequacy and effectiveness of the organization's governance, Risk Management and internal controls
- ✓ Examination and evaluation of the organization's quality of performance in carrying out assigned responsibilities stated goals and objectives

The IAF's responsibilities can include:

- ✓Evaluating risk exposures relating to achievement of the organization's strategic objectives
- ✓Evaluating the reliability and integrity of information and the means used to identify, measure, classify and report such information
- ✓ Evaluating the systems established to ensure compliance with those policies, plans, procedures, laws and regulations which could have a significant impact on the organization
- ✓ Evaluating the means of safeguarding assets and, as appropriate, verifying the existence of such assets
- ✓ Evaluating the effectiveness and efficiency with which resources are employed
- ✓ Monitoring and evaluating governance processes
- ✓ Evaluating operations or programs to ascertain whether results are consistent with established objectives and goals and whether the operations or programs are being carried out as planned
- ✓ Monitoring and evaluating the effectiveness of the organization's Risk Management processes
- ✓ Evaluating the quality of performance of external auditors and the degree of coordination with internal audit
- ✓ Reporting periodically on its own purpose, authority, responsibility and performance relative to its plan
- ✓ Reporting significant risk exposures and control issues, including fraud risks, governance issues and other matters as requested by the Board
- ✓ Evaluating specific operations at the request of the Board or management, as appropriate

1.3.6.3. Why does IAF matter?

Beyond a mechanism for dealing with the agency risk and information asymmetry, internal auditing is also a mechanism by which an organization examines a business process to evaluate its ability to comply with internal and external requirements. Internal audits enable management and Boards to:

- ✓ Discover what's really going on within the organization, which enables more objective decision-making and resource allocation
- ✓ Learn about potential problems before they become burning issues
- ✓ Identify failure points within a process, so relevant stakeholders can implement corrective actions in a timely manner
- ✓ Determine the effectiveness of controls within a process

IAF can be used to bring about improvements in business processes to better meet internal and external requirements. In essence an internal audit is both a compliance tool and an improvement tool.

Consequently, the IAF is one of the cornerstones of Corporate Governance. In its absence, management teams left without internal monitoring can take undue risks and cut corners in ways that undermine the prospects of the business. The IAF is meant to find and escalate critical issues to be heard at the Board. Historically, internal audit has focused on:

- ✓ Financial impact of management actions and omissions
- ✓ Looking at past and current facts
- ✓ Delivering reports on finding on what went or may go wrong based on the status quo

This function is evolving towards more holistic assessments across the business as a whole and including spotting future opportunities and challenges.

It is important to note that creating an effective IAF requires not only commitment from the Board but also human and financial resources. Effective internal auditors are highly qualified professionals with specific personal attributes that enhance their effectiveness. In certain environments such professionals may be hard to find or expensive to hire. A traditional cost benefit analysis for a small and medium-sized enterprise (SME) with limited resources operating in an environment with few qualified auditors in general, may deter a Board of such an SME from introducing an IAF. But it is important to note that traditional cost benefit analysis would not be able to quantify risks that the existence of an IAF would be able to prevent or mitigate. So, despite its cost, the desirability of an IAF increases as the complexity of a business increases and Boards are well advised to commit to its introduction as soon as they deem it even marginally affordable.

1.3.6.4. How do you introduce an IAF?

Introducing an IAF is the responsibility of the oversight body of the business, most commonly the Board of Directors. The Board can mandate the creation of this function and the recruitment of the relevant personnel by the executive management. In turn, and in order to ensure its independence and thus enhance its effectiveness, the internal audit function is directly answerable to the Board. Administratively the IAF reports to the CEO.

The Board or Board Audit Committee typically:

- ✓ Approves the IAF charter
- ✓ Approves the risk based internal audit plan
- ✓ Approves the internal audit budget and resource plan
- ✓ Receives reports from IAF on its performance relative to plan and other matters
- ✓ Approves the hiring and firing of the Internal Auditor
- ✓ Approves the remuneration of the Internal Auditor
- ✓ Seeks to ensure there are no resource limitations or inappropriate scope of activities for IAF

The Internal Auditor will normally communicate and interact directly with the Board, including in executive sessions and between Board meetings with and without the CEO or other senior managers present, as appropriate.

1.3.6.5. Guiding Principles for IAF and its work

There are a number of guiding principles for an IAF and its work.

IAF Independence and Objectivity

This is the first and overriding guiding principle for the IAF and its work. It is imperative that the IAF must remain independent and objective without any interference by any element in the organization on audit selection, scope, procedures, frequency or audit report content. Internal Auditors need to be allowed space, freedom and resources by management to determine these matters for themselves. In order to safeguard their independence and objectivity, Internal Auditors can have no direct operational responsibility or authority over any of the activities audited and they cannot have any involvement in implementing internal controls, developing procedures, installing systems, preparing records or engaging in any other activity that may affect the Internal Auditor's judgement.

They are required to be objective in gathering, evaluating and communicating information about the activity or process being audited. They are also required to provide balanced assessments of all relevant circumstances and not be influenced by their own interests or the interests of others. They are expected to be professional at all times and to confirm the IAF's organizational independence to the Board or Board Audit Committee at least annually.

IAF Internal Audit Plan

Given the importance of internal audits, it is imperative that they are prepared thoroughly and done well. It is therefore an important guiding principle for the IAF that its work is carried out according to an Internal Audit Plan. Such a plan must comprise a work schedule, budget and resource requirements for the period ahead, usually the year ahead. The plan will also prioritize the audits to be conducted based on a risk assessment so that the IAF can focus first on areas and processes with material impact on the business. The IAF or Internal Auditor carrying out the work, needs to periodically review and adjust the plan as necessary in response to internal and external factors. Any significant deviations from the approved Internal Audit Plan would then be communicated to senior management and the Board through periodic activity reports.

IAF reporting and monitoring

A written IAF report is prepared following each internal audit engagement and distributed to the Board or Board Audit Committee and as appropriate to relevant members of the executive management. Such reports will amongst others include a list of nonconformities, their causes and recommended corrective action to deal with them. Ideally, though not always possible, an IAF report will also include management's response and where appropriate corrective action taken or proposed in response to the IAF's findings and recommendations. It is important to note that it is always the management that has the responsibility for identifying and implementing corrective action to clear nonconformities. The IAF on the other hand remains responsible for appropriate follow-up to ensure open issues are cleared by assessing the adequacy and monitoring the implementation of corrective action

In addition to individual internal audit reports, the IAF also needs to report periodically on its own performance relative to plan and at least annually on IAF's purpose, authority and responsibilities as well as on the organization's significant risk exposures and control issues, including fraud risks, governance issues and other matters needed or requested by the management, the Board or the Board Audit Committee.

IAF quality assurance and own improvement program

It would be paradoxical if the function auditing others did not engage in some form of own assessment. Thus, one of the main guiding principles of IAF is for it to maintain a quality assurance and own improvement program that covers all aspects of the IAF. In this context, an IAF needs to evaluate its own adherence to relevant professional body standards, assess its own efficiency and effectiveness and identify opportunities for improvement. In line with its reporting guiding principle, the IAF or Internal Auditor needs to periodically communicate to senior management and the Board or the Board Audit Committee on the IAF's quality assurance and improvement program, including results of ongoing internal assessments and external assessments

1.3.6.6. Key Activities of Internal Audit

There are five key activities of an internal audit

1. Audit scheduling

Audit scheduling addresses:

- ✓ when the organization or a specific part of the organization can expect to be audited
- ✓ Who will lead the auditing effort
- ✓ Which high level processes will be included in the audit

✓ What type of resources may be needed by the management of the process

Audits scheduled far in advance tend to produce better results as the audited entities are better prepared and might even self-correct in anticipation of a forthcoming audit. To the degree that the purpose of an audit is to prevent unwanted outcomes, corrective action taken in anticipation of an audit is to be welcomed.

2. Audit planning

An Audit Plan details a single audit's scope, objectives and agenda and should provide the timetable of the intended audit from start to finish. It should include:

✓ Which specific processes and subprocesses will be audited
✓ Exactly when they will be audited
✓ Who will do the auditing
✓ Which requirements will be audited in each segment

Risk-based audit plans are a common-sense way to planning internal audits as they facilitate the prioritization of audits of areas and processes with greatest risk and potential impact.

3. Audit Management

Managing an audit entails ensuring the audit process stays on track and managing and communicating any changes to the audit plan as well as communicating the audit's progress to the stakeholders. Managing the audit professionally also means reviewing all nonconformities to ensure they are logical, valid and clear. It is imperative there is nothing in the findings that can be perceived as arbitrary. It is incumbent upon the IAF to try and resolve all conflicts constructively and to ensure the entire audit is conducted professionally and positively.

4. Audit reporting

An audit culminates in an audit report which presents the auditors' observations and recommendations. Such a report will at a minimum identify the audited processes, list compliant areas, discuss the degree of compliance, list any nonconformities and discuss causes and potential remedies. An audit report becomes the basis of discussion with management and if needed at Board level.

5. Audit verification

The Audit is meant to lead to confirmation of compliance and identification of nonconformities and relevant corrective action. But it does not stop there. The Audit remains open as long as the findings and nonconformities have not been addressed to the point where there is compliance. Therefore, after the initial report and the response from management to the IAF's findings, there is a further step that needs to be taken by IAF that aims at verifying that compliance has been achieved and nonconformities have been rectified based on corrective action taken as illustrated schematically in the diagram below.

Figure 1.3.6.6.a. Key Internal Audit Activities – Audit Verification

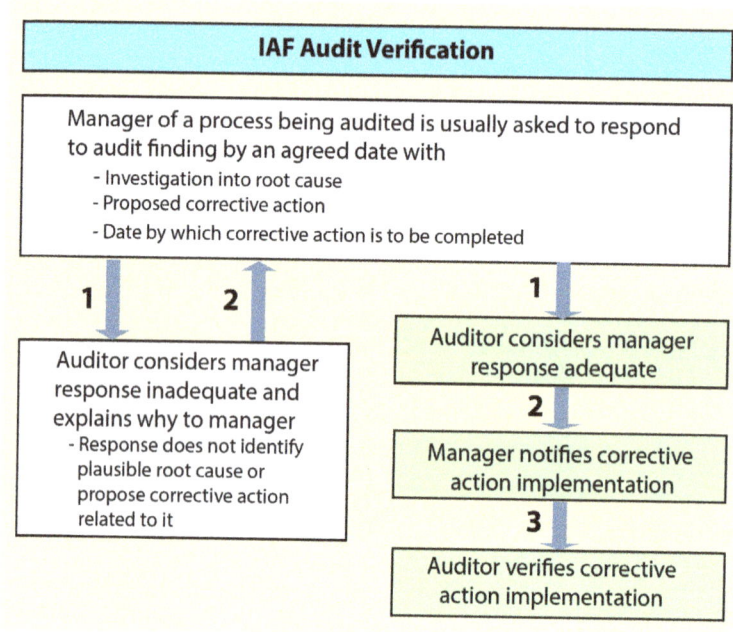

1.3.6.7. Best Practices in IAF

1. Design audits with adequate planning

Planning is required at multiple levels, including strategic regarding the IAF itself and tactical regarding deployment of resources and technology. Audit assignment plans must set out the objectives and scope of the audit to be undertaken as well as the techniques and resources to be used by the auditor. Audit plans need to be formulated with reference to:

- ✓ Nature, size and operation of audited entity
- ✓ Previous audit results and observations
- ✓ Availability and competence of audit staff
- ✓ Audit methodology most suited to the operations being audited
- ✓ Format and general content of audit report to be prepared

2. Ensure appropriate delegation, supervision and staffing of audit function and teams

The IAF must have dedicated staff with an appropriate mix of experience, expertise and people skills. Internal auditors must have sufficient proficiency and training to carry out the tasks delegated to them. Supervision within the IAF should be used to ensure quality control through:

- ✓ Providing instructions in creating and in approving or recommending approval of the audit program
- ✓ Ensuring the audit program is completed, unless deviations are both justified and authorized
- ✓ Determining that the working papers adequately support the audit findings, conclusions and reports
- ✓ Making sure audit reports are accurate, objective, clear, concise, constructive and timely
- ✓ Determining that the audit objectives are being met

3. Carry out systematic evaluation of controls

Internal controls comprise plans and methods adopted to safeguard assets, comply with laws and regulations, ensure completeness and correctness of accounting data, promote efficiency and promote adherence to management policies. The IAF must systematically evaluate the nature of the operation and system of controls of the audited entity to assess the reliance that can be placed on these controls. In doing so, the IAF needs to prioritize and focus its review on controls that have an important bearing on the reliability of the audited entity, system or process. A satisfactory control system will exhibit, amongst others:

✓ Proper segregation of functional responsibilities
✓ A system of authorization, recording and procedures adequate to provide accounting control over assets, liabilities, revenues and expenses
✓ Sound practices in performance of duties and functions of the organization units

4. Formulate opinions based on sufficient information and proper evidence

Acceptance of the IAF's reports relies on such reports and opinions expressed in them being beyond reproach of charges of arbitrariness and/or bias. Therefore, best practice calls for internal auditors to obtain all of the information and evidence considered necessary for the expression of an informed opinion and lay out such information and evidence in detail and in support of the internal auditors' opinions and findings. Of course the evidence required will vary and an experienced auditor must sometimes use professional judgment to determine the amount and nature of the evidence required with reference to the:

✓ Nature of the item under examination
✓ Materiality of possible errors or irregularities
✓ Degree of risk involved, which is largely dependent on the adequacy of the internal controls
✓ Susceptibility of the given item to conversion, manipulation or misstatement

5. Maintain high standard working papers

Maintaining high standard working papers is an important best practice and serves multiple purposes:

✓ Assist directly in the performance of the audit
✓ Provide a historical record of the audit work
✓ Contain the basis for the auditor's opinion
✓ Provide information for the auditor's report
✓ Aid the review and evaluation of the audit work
✓ Support action if necessary by providing evidentiary documentation

6. Undertake regular quality reviews

Maintaining standards requires regular quality reviews. Such reviews need to examine the preparation, review and approval of IAF field plans. They need to ensure that the direction, supervision and review of work at all levels is adequate and that working papers comply with the standards prescribed. Such reviews also need to ensure that significant issues are properly documented, pursued to finality and reported appropriately. The reviews are also an opportunity to resolve any differences of professional judgment among staff involved in audits. Overall, the review process is a mechanism for ensuring the quality of each audit meets appropriate professional standards.

7. Ensure full and continuous management and Board support for IAF

We have already examined the need for IAF to have a direct reporting relationship to the Board via the Board Audit Committee and the need to have sufficient autonomy from the management to carry out its audit work without interference. Both the management and the Board have a responsibility to ensure the IAF has adequate resources, both human and other to carry out its function to a high standard. The attitude of management towards IAF sets the tone for and can have a significant influence on the behaviour of an organization's staff towards the IAF. The Board on the other hand must ensure the IAF's independence and standing within the organization. Without full and continuous support from both management and the Board, the IAF will not deliver optimal performance.

8. Use appropriate internal controls questionnaires

One of the tools used by internal auditors are internal controls questionnaires (ICQs) which are examined in detail in the next section. Carefully developing and deploying such ICQs is an important best practice for the IAF.

1.3.6.8. ICQs tool for Internal Audit

We have already encountered Internal Risk Controls under Risk Management and how, they can, when working effectively, contribute to alleviating risk and promoting the prospects of the business attaining its objectives. We have also seen how the absence of, or weak Internal Risk Controls can increase risk (Section 1.3.5.6). As with any other aspect of the functioning of the business, Internal Risk Controls can be the subject of an Internal Audit, seeking to ensure they are fit for purpose and working effectively in practice. Such an internal audit of Internal Risk Controls can use the ICQ tool, which when well prepared and targeted can form part of an effective internal audit.

An ICQ is a series of "Yes" or "No" questions about the internal controls under audit examination. "Yes" means the needed control or policy is in place and "No" means the needed control or policy is absent and risk is enhanced. Yes/No answers to such questions need confirmation through testing before being accepted. The ICQs need to be customized to the specifics of the entity or operation being audited. A list of areas for which customized ICQs may be advisable is provided in Annex 1 and we see some sample parts of generic ICQs for certain areas below:

Sample part of generic ICQ – policies & procedures

➤ Does your department have an up-to-date copy of the department's policies and procedures manual?
➤ Are written policies and procedures maintained for all departmental functions?
➤ Are these policies and procedures reviewed and updated annually?
➤ Does your department have an organizational chart that clearly defines lines of authority and responsibility?
➤ Are current job descriptions on file for each employee in the department?

Sample part of generic ICQ – petty cash

➤ Are petty cash funds kept in secure storage?
➤ Are there policies on the use of petty cash funds?
➤ Are policies on the use of petty cash followed?
➤ Do all petty cash disbursements require original receipts for reimbursement?
➤ Are surprise cash counts of department petty cash funds performed on a regular, random or unannounced basis?

Sample part of generic ICQ – IT security

➤ Is the need for password security reinforced to all staff?

> ➤ Is the use of software not licensed to the department or organization prohibited on department or organization computers?
> ➤ Are computer applications logged off when the user is away from the computer?
> ➤ Are all storage media brought in from outside sources tested for computer viruses before being used?
> ➤ Is back-up storage maintained of all critical information?
> ➤ Is sensitive information password protected?
> ➤ Are electrical surge suppressers used on all computer equipment?
> ➤ Are staff encouraged to save work frequently?

1.3.6.9. Drivers for IAF effectiveness

As a service function dealing with other parts of the organization, the effectiveness of the IAF depends crucially on the attributes of the internal auditors themselves. In this context there are certain key attributes that are essential for internal auditors to possess. These include:

- ✓ Integrity – being honest and fair so audit reports are considered trustworthy, fair and reliable
- ✓ Objectivity – assessing facts with the utmost care and refraining from reckless and irresponsible statements or resorting to expressions without proper evidence
- ✓ Competency/professional knowledge – applying appropriate skill and knowledge combined with adequate experience and undertake projects within his/her scope of skills and competence
- ✓ Confidentiality – safeguarding all information gathered as part of audit process without spill out unless there is statutory, legal or professional requirement to do so
- ✓ Independence – being able to report on material facts and figures, uninfluenced by any favour or frown

These attributes mean that high quality internal auditors need both soft skills such as sound judgment, enquiring mindset, relationship building capabilities, management skills and communication skills, and hard skills such as professional knowledge and competence, analytical capability, problem solving and solution-oriented expertise, in order to be effective. They must also be resilient in dealing with audited entities, management and the Board during the audit process, in issuing audit reports and in post report monitoring and follow-up.

An effective internal audit program creates a feedback loop:

- ✓ Internal audit takes a snapshot of the current environment and identifies nonconformities or opportunities for improvement
- ✓ Management in consultation with IAF design and implement corrective action
- ✓ IAF verifies the corrective action has been implemented and the cause of the original nonconformity has been eliminated
- ✓ Management and Board support and commitment to IAF's role underpins effective IAF activity with audit and corrective action process institutionalized

Figure 1.3.6.9.a. Feedback benefits from effective IAF

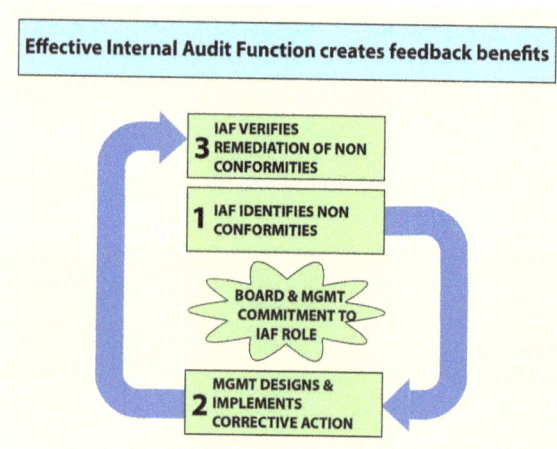

Effective Internal Audit Function creates feedback benefits

3 IAF VERIFIES REMEDIATION OF NON CONFORMITIES

1 IAF IDENTIFIES NON CONFORMITIES

BOARD & MGMT. COMMITMENT TO IAF ROLE

2 MGMT DESIGNS & IMPLEMENTS CORRECTIVE ACTION

IAF delivers good results when organizations can answer key questions:

- ✓ Are the processes and metrics clearly defined, so internal audit process can discover unambiguous nonconformance?
- ✓ How does the audit process incorporate the results of previous audits to track progress against previously discovered nonconformities?
- ✓ What is the process to identify potential root causes in a timely manner for the nonconformities that are discovered by the audit process?

✓ Are corrective actions always taken to eliminate root causes or potential root causes of nonconformities?

✓ How is the data on corrective and preventive actions reported and analyzed?

✓ How do employees receive feedback on their respective nonconformities?

1.3.7. Management Information Systems and Key Performance Indicators

1.3.7.1. What are Management Information Systems and Key Performance Indicators?

Earlier sections have examined the need for relevant and timely information materials for the Board as well as data to facilitate risk analysis and Risk Management. Internal audit also requires availability of data and information. A Management Information Systems (MIS) is the organized integration of hardware and software technologies, data, processes and human elements that ensures relevant and timely information and data capture, analysis, storage and availability for the users of such information and data in the organization in their decision-making processes. These users can include the Board and the senior management as well as line managers depending on the data and information concerned.

A Key Performance Indicator (KPI) is a measurable value that demonstrates how effectively a company is achieving key business objectives. Organizations use KPIs at multiple levels to evaluate their success at reaching targets. KPIs are an example of what a MIS can generate for the Board or senior management of a company.

Both MIS and KPIs are tools that can be used by different layers of management in a company as well as the Board of Directors of a company to better inform their decision-making. In this sense, they are a valuable set of tools that promotes better Corporate Governance.

1.3.7.2. Components, Objectives and Characteristics of MIS

An MIS at a minimum requires people and data. The interaction of these two components in a systematic way can be a rudimentary management information system. For example, before computers were invented, a clerk could keep count of inventory manually in a warehouse and issue a report to reorder supplies when the inventory reached a set level. The advent of computers and radio-frequency identification (RFID) technology has removed the need for a clerk to do manual stocktaking and provide a report as the level of inventories can be monitored remotely in real time through scanning and computer technologies. In this type of example, the reordering is often also computerized as well. The MIS provides a report of all this that is used by the supervisor or manager of the warehouse. And the MIS has moved from the simple clerk issued report prompting action, to a system integrating hardware technologies (computers, RFID and scanning equipment) and software technologies, data and people resources.

As our example illustrated, the main objectives of an MIS are to:

1. Capture relevant data
2. Process the data into information that can be useful to authorized users
3. Store the information for later use by authorized users
4. Allow retrieval of the information by authorized users
5. Disseminate the information in appropriate format and in timely fashion to authorized users

What distinguishes an MIS from an ad-hoc approach to data gathering and use is that it is characterized by the following:

- ✓ System approach – there is an architecture and a method to the way an MIS is organized so it behaves like a robust system
- ✓ Management oriented – the design of an MIS starts with the determination of management needs and overall business objectives
- ✓ Need based – an MIS aims to cater to the needs of managers at different levels of a business.
- ✓ Exceptions based – in any abnormal situation, when values recorded are at maximum, minimum or outside tolerance limits, there should be an exception report generated to the decision-maker at the relevant level
- ✓ Future oriented – besides exception-based reporting, MIS should also look at the future and in addition to past or historical information, it should also provide projections which can catalyze review or debate and possibly action at relevant levels in the business

✓ Integrated – when designing and implementing an MIS, it is vitally important to properly integrate all relevant data and sources of such data so the information coming out of the MIS is based on a holistic approach that takes all relevant facts and data into account at any given time

✓ Long-term planning – MISs take time to design and implement and cannot be changed quickly. It is therefore critical that the long-term needs and objectives of the business are kept in mind when introducing MIS

✓ Modular architecture – modular architecture where subsystems can be self-contained can help keep the overall MIS less cumbersome and allow implementation and updates in future in modularized or incremental ways

✓ Centralized database and warehousing – it is generally more efficient to gather data once, validate it properly and then store it centrally for use by individual sub-systems

1.3.7.3. Role, Benefits, Costs and Limitations of MIS

An MIS is a versatile Corporate Governance tool that plays an important facilitating role in business organizations including in:

✓ Decision making – in any organization, decisions are made on the basis of relevant information and a well-designed and functioning MIS can provide high quality information in timely fashion to assist in decision-making.

✓ Performance monitoring – in any business, it is part of the Board's and the senior management's responsibility to monitor performance. An MIS can perform the function of keeping score and facilitating performance monitoring.

✓ Identifying areas in need of attention – in any business environment any mistakes or unintended or unwanted deviations from expected performance and outcomes, whichever way they happen to arise, can be easier to deal with if they are flagged in a timely fashion. Once again, given an MIS's capacity to capture and provide information about every aspect of the business, one of the key uses of an MIS is to help flag areas in need of attention in a timely manner and before they evolve into something more serious.

✓ Formulating strategy – strategy formulation requires good quality information which is much more difficult to collect and present to the Board of a company that is seeking to formulate strategy, in the absence of a well-designed and functioning MIS.

Figure 1.3.7.3.a. MISs Role in Corporate Governance

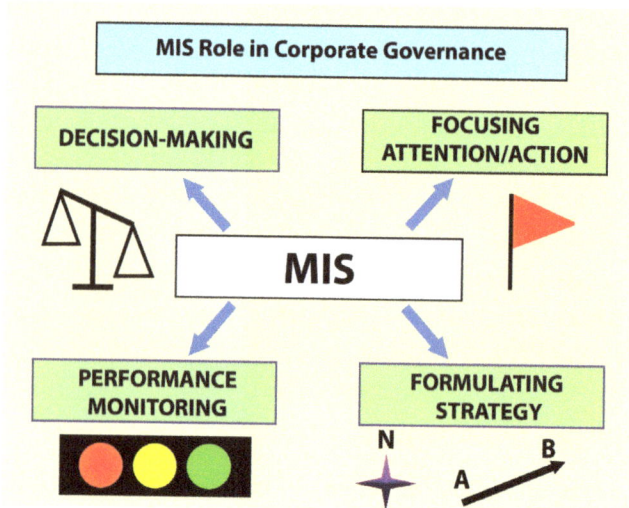

Given the role an MIS can play, the benefits from a well-designed and well-functioning MIS in terms of Corporate Governance include improved quantity and quality of information for decision-making, performance monitoring, troubleshooting and strategy formulation. Of course an MIS can also have significant benefits for the day-to-day management of a business including, among others:

✓ Improved quality and quantity of management decisions
✓ Improved quality of internal and external communications as they can leverage more and better quality information
✓ Improved quality of planning
✓ Improved operational flexibility and efficiency

MISs can require significant investment, particularly when a new computer based system is to be introduced. There is also usually a need to train staff which adds to the cost and ongoing overheads. Once introduced an MIS also requires maintenance and periodic updates which add to its cost. Taking all into account, an MIS can require significant investment. Indeed an MIS can sometimes be perceived as an expensive luxury. However, the cost does not have to be prohibitive and smart ways of designing and implementing an MIS (e.g. modular) means a business can begin with a narrower MIS which meets critical needs and expands over time.

Even though an MIS has significant benefits which we have discussed above, it also has its limitations. The most obvious of these is that while an MIS may help solve some critical problems, it is not a solution to all problems of an organization. Moreover, it cannot meet the special demands of every potential user. Even if designed well, an MIS will also be of limited value if the basic data is obsolete or outdated. The adage "garbage in, garbage out", needs to be kept in mind to ensure the input data is of sufficient quality to allow MIS to serve its purpose. Of course the opposite problem can also create limitations for the use of an MIS, i.e. if the MIS is designed in an improper manner then even good quality data will not allow it to serve management's needs and will end up being considered irrelevant and a waste of resources.

A criticism that is often levelled at MISs is that they provide information mostly in quantitative form. However, there is nothing that precludes qualitative information from being part of regular MIS reports to management and the Board. In fact, a good MIS includes some degree of commentary, including qualitative, of the "numbers". Like any tool, an MIS does have limitations but its true usefulness is determined by the way it is designed, implemented and used.

1.3.7.4. A case study of the role and value of an MIS in a transition economy

In early 1996, the European Bank for Reconstruction and Development (EBRD), a multilateral financial institution, made an equity investment in a Russian railway leasing company and the funds were used to expand the company's fleet of specialized heated tank-wagons which were used to transport Russian petrochemical products to export markets. The governance rights negotiated for the EBRD included representation at the company's Board of Directors and the author was nominated to serve on the Board. Despite having a good internal accounting department and international external auditors, the company lacked a formal MIS. The author prioritized the introduction of a formal MIS that would allow monthly financial reporting for the management and the Board. This was implemented at some expense with help from the external auditors of the company and by early 1997 the Board was receiving monthly management accounts within ten days from the end of each month. In 1997, the volume of Russian petrochemical exports rose and the company's heated tank-wagons were in great demand and profits rose sharply. In 1998, the price of oil dropped very sharply during the first half of the year. Demand for the company's tank wagons declined precipitously as Russian exporters decided to reduce their exports of petrochemical products and export crude oil instead. Because the MIS was in place and already working well, the Board and the management were able to monitor almost in real time the impact of this dislocation in the oil markets on the company's profitability, cashflow and balance sheet. As a result, the Board initiated discussions with the General Director in June 1998 urging him to develop and present to the Board an urgent cost-cutting and turnaround plan for implementation in the second half of 1998. As a result of the Board's timely request for action, the General Director developed and implemented an action plan which allowed the company to reverse the steep losses already incurred in the first half of 1998 and break even for the year before returning to profitability once again in 1999 and with its balance sheet still strong. If the MIS had not been in place and providing monthly financial management accounts, it is doubtful whether the management and the Board would have been able to take action in as timely and effective manner.

1.3.7.5. Designing effective KPIs

KPIs are often the output of an MIS. They are a form of communication and they need to be succinct, clear and relevant if they are to be understood and acted upon. Thus, formulating an individual KPI requires a good understanding of the objectives the indicator will be used to measure, how you plan to achieve these objectives and who can act based on the KPI. It also requires the involvement and feedback of multiple parties (e.g. business analysts, department heads, senior managers) and is often an iterative process. As the name implies, the operative word is "key" because every KPI should be related to a specific and important business outcome with a performance measure. Considering answers to the following questions can help in the design of a KPI:

➤ What is your desired outcome?
➤ Why does this outcome matter?
➤ How are you going to measure progress?
➤ How can you influence the outcome?
➤ Who is responsible for the business outcome?
➤ How will you know you've achieved your outcome?
➤ How often will you review progress towards the outcome?

For example, if the objective is to increase sales, then a sales growth KPI might be defined through addressing the questions above as below:

➤ To increase sales for this year by 25% relative to last year's sales
➤ Achieving this target will allow the business to double its profits
➤ Progress will be measured as an increase in revenue
➤ By offering promotions to customers and making the product available through additional channels of distribution
➤ The Marketing Director will be responsible for this metric
➤ Sales will have increased by 25% this year relative to last year's sales
➤ Will be reviewed on a monthly basis

One way to evaluate the relevance of a performance indicator is to use the SMART criteria. The letters stand for or **Specific, Measurable, Attainable, Relevant, Time-bound**. In other words:

✓ Is your objective **Specific**? If it is not, then there could be ambiguity in its measurement.
✓ Can you **Measure** progress towards that goal? If it is not possible to measure progress then there is the risk you will not be able to make any timely adjustments on the way if you are falling short.
✓ Is the goal realistically **Attainable**? If it is not, then the KPI is being set up from the start to measure degrees of failure which is of limited use.
✓ How **Relevant** is the goal to your organization? If it is not, then monitoring if it is achieved or not will not have any actionable value to anyone.
✓ What is the **Time-frame** for achieving this goal? If there is no specific time-frame identified, there will be uncertainty in the timing of measurement.

The SMART criteria can also be expanded to be SMARTER with the addition of **Evaluate** and **Re-evaluate**. These two steps are extremely important, as they ensure the continuous assessment of KPIs and their relevance to the business. For example, if a sales target for the current year has been met or been exceeded, it becomes important to determine whether that was because the target was set at too low a level to begin with or its achievement is genuinely attributable to related initiatives which the business may have taken.

Figure 1.3.7.5.a. Designing SMART and SMARTER Key Performance Indicators

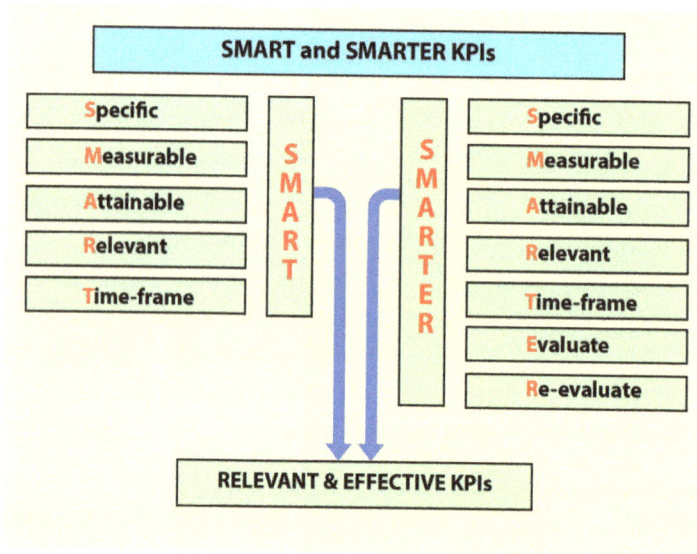

KPIs should be considered as a dynamic tool which need to evolve and change as conditions and objectives change in order to remain relevant.

1.3.7.6. Use and benefits of KPIs

KPIs are often thought of as tools reserved for a company's Board of Directors, CEO and other senior managers who make important strategic decisions. This is indeed one of the main utilities of KPIs through the KPI reports and KPI dashboards which provide their recipients with snapshots of performance along multiple KPIs and help them better understand the performance and condition of the business as well as any trends affecting the business. Given that KPIs are by definition designed with the key strategic objectives of the business in mind, the KPI reports and KPI dashboards are also a means of monitoring the management's progress in delivering on the implementation of the company's strategy. Thus, one key benefit from the use of KPIs at senior management and Board level is how their decision-making can be better informed as a result of such use.

Thoughtfully developed KPIs also generate benefits through the process by which they are designed. When disciplined this process forces the organization to be clear and focused on key objectives and invites employee engagement as well. Such employee engagement is in itself a significant benefit. Moreover, the adoption of specific KPIs communicates the strategic priorities of the business to all staff in a way that allows them to recognize and feel connected to the important end goals of the organization, much more than discussion of strategy documents and presentations. This is another aspect of employee engagement which benefits the business. Finally, staff know that what gets measured and monitored also gets rewarded when achieved. KPIs are therefore a powerful signalling device from management to staff as to what are the goals and expectations that should drive their efforts.

1.3.8. Code of Conduct

1.3.8.1. What is a Code of Conduct?

A Code of Conduct is a written document through which a company seeks to articulate for its internal use, as well as external dissemination, the values, rules, principles and behavioural guidelines within which it commits itself and its employees to operate. It provides guidance to employees, customers and other stakeholders as to what the company considers valued and desirable in interactions and relationships. It is sometimes also called a Code of Business Standards or a Code of Ethics. In some cases, depending on the business model applicable to a company, Codes of Conduct are also intended to apply to suppliers and sub-contractors.

A Code of Conduct aims to define how employees should behave in carrying out their duties. Thus it reflects a company's operations, core values and overall company culture. It is clearly an element and a tool of Corporate Governance as the principles that such a code commits the company and its workforce to, reflect the values and mission set for the company by its shareholders, Board and management. As a result, every Code of Conduct is unique to the company it serves.

1.3.8.2. Why does a Code of Conduct matter?

As a tool and an element of Corporate Governance, a Code of Conduct sets the bar in respect of the company's expectations regarding ethical behaviour, conformity with laws and regulatory compliance. It also provides employees with a reference guide in the event they encounter ethical dilemmas or generally find themselves in situations where the correct course of action is not immediately obvious. It is also a very powerful communication tool which explains to internal and external audiences alike what the company stands for and the parameters within which it is prepared to conduct its business, hence the name.

Whilst the absence of a Code of Conduct does not preclude appropriately ethical behaviour, its presence removes or at least reduces the likelihood of excuses for transgressions by employees on the grounds that they did not know or understand the parameters within which they were meant to carry out their duties. Indeed, clear articulation and communication of a Code of Conduct can facilitate the use of the legal doctrine of a "faithless servant", in cases where an employee knowingly engages in misconduct in violation of the employer's Code of Conduct. In Morgan Stanley vs. Skowron (2013) a New York court applied this doctrine and sanctioned the claw back of millions in compensation from an employee who had been engaged in insider trading in violation of his company's Code of Conduct, which also required him to report his misconduct.

Of course setting the ground rules clearly provides some protection to employees too, particularly if they are ever asked or encouraged by their superiors to act outside these ground rules. Typically, a robust Code of Conduct will include both whistleblowing protections and escalation channels that ensure employees do not feel pressured to stray from the Code of Conduct and are able to report misconduct by others as they become aware of it.

Whilst Codes of Conduct are important to all types of companies, such codes are especially relevant to companies with valuable brands. The image of a consumer-facing company is often intertwined with the product or service they deliver to their customers and it is often an important consideration in how customers choose clothes, shoes, cars, smartphones and other goods. Even a suspicion of unethical practices can be deleterious to a brand. Not surprisingly some of the most comprehensive Codes of Conduct come from consumer-facing companies who own some of the biggest brands. Moreover, some of these companies extend their Codes of Conduct to their suppliers and subcontractors, particularly where the nature of their business model includes significant outsourcing and integration of parts from suppliers in countries where regulatory frameworks and their implementation may not be as robust as in their primary consumer markets. In this context, Codes of Conduct serve also as powerful marketing documents and their visual appeal becomes a factor in their effectiveness.

1.3.8.3. Typical elements of a Code of Conduct

A typical Code of Conduct begins with a statement from the company's Chairman or CEO setting out the company's commitment to conduct its business with integrity in accordance with ethical standards and in full compliance of all relevant laws, regulations, contractual obligations and internal policies. This statement may also include explicit undertaking against specific illegal acts such as discrimination, harassment. In addition, the opening statement usually provides an explanation of why a Code of Conduct is being introduced and stresses how important is individual employee compliance for the achievement of the company's mission and business goals.

The topics that are typically covered and for which a code will usually provide guidance through prescriptive language and possibly also with what if situational examples, usually include, among others:

- ✓ Strict compliance with laws, rules and regulations
- ✓ Avoidance of conflicts of interest and guidelines for how to deal with conflicts of interest if and when they arise
- ✓ Guidelines on how to treat confidential information and restrictions on use of company information by employees for personal benefit
- ✓ Commitment to fair dealing with customers and suppliers and avoidance of any anti-trust activity or collusion with competitors
- ✓ Strict prohibition of engaging in any bribery or other forms of corruption of any third party
- ✓ Ongoing commitment to protect company assets, including intellectual property and trade secrets
- ✓ Ongoing vigilance against fraud and theft by employees and any counterparties
- ✓ Explicit commitment to sustainability and diversity in pursuit of the company's business goals

✓ Reporting obligations and procedures for noncompliance and whistleblowing protections

✓ Clear accountability provisions specifying consequences for breach of policy and unethical conduct in violation of the code

As it is impossible for any Code of Conduct, however comprehensive it may be, to cover all scenarios that employees may encounter, it is vitally important that a Code of Conduct makes clear how employees should seek advice and guidance when they are unsure of their duties and obligations under their company's code. Escalation channels and methods should be clearly identified in a Code of Conduct so employees can know who to turn for such advice and guidance form an important safeguard mechanism for the code. A code that does not flag the possibility and methods for escalation in case of doubt would be leaving employees to their own devices and increase the risk of them straying from the code.

1.3.8.4. How do you introduce a Code of Conduct?

A Code of Conduct is a tool with considerable reflexivity as it is shaped by the circumstances of the company it serves whilst at the same time, it can influence the future of the company. Whilst it can change as circumstances, external and internal to the company evolve, it is nevertheless also intended to act as a constant beacon for at least a period of time. Consequently, it is important for the owners, Board and management of a company to take time to develop and introduce the Code of Conduct that best serves their company.

The formulation of a Code of Conduct will typically be a task that is carried out by the management of a company but under the watchful supervision of its Board of Directors who ultimately carry the responsibility for its approval. A small taskforce which will include employees with significant experience of the company's operations and daily activities and representatives of the legal, marketing and human resources departments, reporting to the company's CEO, is usually given the responsibility of preparing a draft Code of Conduct. External experts in Corporate Governance may also be involved in the drafting phase. The Code is eventually approved by the Board of the company and then disseminated internally and externally.

The factors that usually influence the drafting of such a code include:

- ✓ The company's own culture, values and mission
- ✓ Cultural and legal norms in the country or countries where the company operates
- ✓ Standards expected by customers in the company's main markets
- ✓ Practices already established by competitors in the company's main markets

As Codes of Conduct are public documents, there are a lot of examples of Codes of Conduct from established companies, including listed companies, that owners, Boards and management teams can study and learn from. A list of some examples of such Codes of Conduct is provided in Annex 2.

In practical terms a Code needs to be written for the reader in language that is accessible and free from technical or legal jargon. If the company operates in multiple jurisdictions, it should be published in the languages of its countries of operations and in a language that takes into account the education and experience level of line employees. It needs to cover all the important areas that may impact the working lives of employees and provide or at least suggest how to get answers to common questions that arise. It is vitally important that the senior management of the company is fully committed to the code and the foreword from the company's CEO is an important signal to that effect. Of course it must be readily accessible to all employees and other stakeholders. Many companies include the Code or links to the code in their annual report or their websites.

Publishing the Code and educating the workforce is only the first step in using the Code as a tool of Corporate Governance. Beyond that a company also needs to ensure employees comprehend the standards expected of them and to reinforce these standards in practice every day. Thus, a company should periodically audit its own employees' understanding of the key elements of the code, through seminars and scenario based ethical dilemma tests. In cases where the code is intended to also cover the activities of subcontractors and suppliers, such auditing and even more robust monitoring needs to be extended to them through site visits, including unannounced ones.

Finally in the event of violations of the Code by employees or subcontractors or suppliers, management must undertake timely action. Experience shows that organizations that do not respond to violations of basic values invite further violations and risk fostering an environment where ethics exit in writing but are ignored in practice. In order to guard against that, when violations are identified there should not only be action in response of the violations but also communication of the actions taken and use of lessons learnt to reinforce training of employees understanding of the Code and of the importance of adherence to the Code.

1.3.9. Innovation and the Strategy Cycle

It may appear strange to include a section focused on innovation and strategy cycle in a chapter devoted to Corporate Governance. But, in our view it would have been stranger if such a section was not included. After all, both innovation and the frequency or cycle of strategy formulation play a big role in how a company allocates resources and in our view good Corporate Governance includes the prudent management of the process by which resources are allocated in order to promote the longevity of the business. We consider therefore why and how companies need to embrace innovation as good Corporate Governance. And we examine how the sector in which the company operates affects the strategic review cycle. We further examine how the two elements can be made to interact with each other in a disciplined way which we consider good Corporate Governance.

1.3.9.1. Embracing innovation as part of good Corporate Governance

It is a commonly known and accepted fact that most broad stock indices are quite dynamic when it comes to their constituent companies. Indeed, a simple examination of the components of the Dow Jones Industrial over the last 60 years shows that only one of the components of this index in 1959, the Procter & Gamble Company, is still in the index. From the components of the index in 1991, there are nine that remain in the index today (Procter & Gamble, 3M, American Express, Coca-Cola, IBM, JP Morgan, McDonald's, Merck and Disney). Five of today's Dow components were formed after 1975 (Microsoft (1975), Apple (1976), Amgen (1980), Verizon (1983), Cisco (1984)).

Table 1.3.9.1.a. Historical composition of Dow Jones Industrial Average Index

Dow Jones Index Components

#	1959	1976	1991	2005	2020
1	Allied Chemical Corporation	Allied Chemical Corporation	Allied Signal Inc	3M Company	3M Company
2	Aluminium Company of America	Aluminium Company of America	Aluminium Company of America	Alcoa Inc.	American Express Company
3	American Can Company	American Can Company	American Expres	Altria Goup Inc.	Amgen Inc.
4	American Telephone & Telegraph Company	American Telephone & Telegraph Company	American Telephone & Telegraph Company	American Express Company	Apple Inc.
5	American Tobacco Company	American Tobacco Company	Bethlehem Steel Corporation	American International Group	Boeing Company
6	Anaconda Mining Company	Bethlehem Steel Corporation	Boeing Company	AT&T	Caterpillar
7	Bethlehem Steel Corporation	Chrysler Corporation	Caterpillar Inc	Boeing Company	Chevron Corporation
8	Chrysler Corporation	E.I.duPont	Chevron Corporation	Caterpillar	Cisco
9	E.I.duPont	Eastman Kodak Company	Coca-Cola Company	Citigroup	Coca-Cola
10	Eastman Kodak Company	Esmark Corporation (ex Swift & Company)	E.I.duPont	Coca-Cola	Dow
11	General Electric Company	Exxon (ex Standard Oil Co of New Jersey)	Eastman Kodak Company	E.I.duPont	Goldman Sachs
12	General Foods Company	General Electric Company	Exxon	ExxonMobil	Home Depot
13	General Motors Company	General Foods Company	General Electric Company	General Electric Company	Honeywell
14	Goodyear Tire & Rubber Company	General Motors Company	General Motors Company	General Motors Company	Intel
15	International Harverster Company	Goodyear Tire & Rubber Company	Goodyear Tire & Rubber Company	Hewlet Packard	IBM
16	International Nickel Company	Inco (ex International Nickel Company)	IBM	Home Depot	Johson & Johnson
17	International Paper Company	International Harvester Company	International Paper Company	Honeywell	JP Morgan
18	Johns-Manville Corporation	International Paper Company	JP Morgan Company	Intel	McDonald's
19	Owens Illinois Inc	Johns-Manville Corporation	McDonald's Corporation	IBM	Merck & Co
20	The Procter & Gamble Company	Minessota Mining & Manufacturing Company	Merck & Co Inc	Johson & Johnson	Microsoft
21	Sears Roebuck & Company	Owens Illinois Inc	Minessota Mining & Manufacturing Company	JP Morgan	Nike
22	Standard Oil Co of California	The Procter & Gamble Company	Philip Morris Companies	McDonalds	Procter & Gamble
23	Standard Oil Co of New Jersey	Sears Roebuck & Company	The Procter & Gamble Company	Merck & Co	Salesforce
24	Swift & Company	Standard Oil Co of California	Sears Roebuck & Company	Microsoft	Travellers
25	Texaco Inc.	Texaco Inc.	Texaco Inc.	Pfizer	United Health
26	Union Carbide Corporation	Union Carbide Corporation	Union Carbide Corporation	Procter & Gamble	Verizon
27	United Aircraft Corporation	United States Steel Corporation	United Technologies (ex United Aircraft Corpn)	United Technologies (ex Aircraft Corpn)	Visa
28	United States Steel Corporation	United Technologies (ex United Aircraft Corpn)	Walt DInsey Company	Verizon Communications	Walgreens Boots Alliance
29	Westinghouse Electric Corporation	Westinghouse Electric Corporation	Westinghouse Electric Corporation	WalMart	WalMart
30	F.W.Woolworth	F.W.Woolworth	F.W.Woolworth	Walt Disney	Walt Disney

Similar patterns (though not exactly the same percentages) are observable from other, broader indices in the US and indices in other countries (e.g. UK, France, Germany, etc.) In short, companies drop out of the indices as they get taken over, merge or fail and other companies grow to replace them. This is often accepted as a fact of life, presented as proof of the dynamism of market economies and explained as an inevitable consequence of technological advances which enable challenger companies with winning new technologies to overtake established ones with old technologies.

Given the way stock markets are discounting future cashflows, one can also argue that the components of the main indices at any given point in time, reflect the investors' expectations about the future cashflows of different companies and sectors. So, the relegation of individual company stocks from elite indices and elevation of other individual stocks to replace them also reflects secular rotation of investor interest into and out of different sectors of economic activity. Analysis of the Dow Jones components by sector confirms that at certain times certain sectors get overrepresented and at other times other sectors get overrepresented as can be seen below.

Table 1.3.9.1.b. Dow Jones components – partial sector analysis

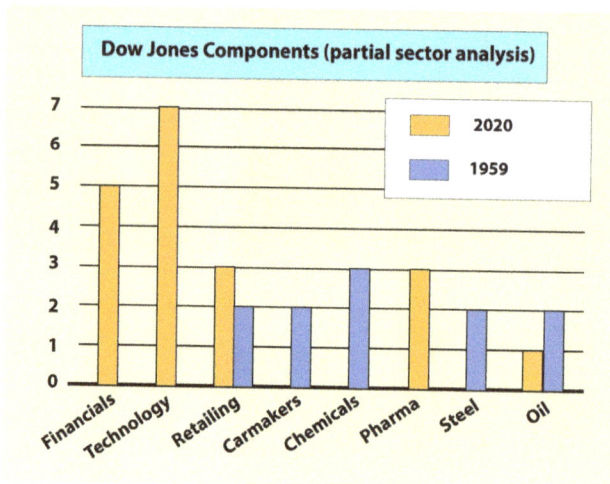

All the above raise an important question for Boards and owners of companies to consider. How can a company improve its prospects of longevity in the face of all of the above? We feel the answer is to be sensitive to change and be prepared to change themselves so their products or services remain relevant and attractive to existing and new customers in sufficient numbers to underpin continued viability. In short, we consider embracing innovation as one of the keys to longevity.

Embracing innovation as a necessary condition to remain competitive may appear obvious for companies in certain sectors. For example, pharmaceutical companies have long been understood as requiring both distribution capabilities for their existing products and a pipeline of future products in order to attract high and sustainable ratings from analysts and investors. Similarly, companies engaged in consumer electronics are also expected to build today's products and invent the products of tomorrow. In such companies, investment in research and development is understood as tantamount to investment in the future of the companies themselves. But, whilst we recognize the importance of investment in research and development and its link to innovation, we believe the term innovation itself needs to be considered as an umbrella concept that may go beyond the laboratory and technology. By way of example, we note that selling spinach pie at a kiosk at the Athens international airport may not appear to be particularly innovative. After all, there is nothing more quintessentially Greek than the humble spinach pie and the Greek saying "You haven't invented the spinach pie" is often used to derisively dismiss claims of inventiveness and innovation. But, when it is McDonald's selling spinach pie on the menu of its kiosk in Athens airport alongside its traditional hamburgers, or beer in its restaurants in Belgium, or other local favourites in its restaurants in other parts of the world, one must acknowledge that it demonstrates a certain willingness and readiness to consider the menu in innovative ways so that it continues to appeal to local tastes. It is not surprising to also see McDonald's being prepared to experiment with its menus and to even add meat substitute burgers next to its traditional beef ones. This willingness to innovate certainly contributes to McDonald's longevity and continued success.

But innovation and sustained investment in research and development is not a guarantee by itself for longevity. Consider the example of Kodak.

In its heyday, Kodak was one of the most innovative companies around with many patents for new technologies invented in its laboratories. Yet, Kodak failed to remain a thriving business. Its products lost their technological advantage even as Kodak kept getting more patents. What went wrong? Sadly, its research and development efforts appear to have been directed in areas where Kodak itself could not take advantage in its core business. And so whilst undoubtedly resources were indeed allocated to support innovation, the innovation that was taking place was not relevant to Kodak's own product offerings and customers.

A fourth company that was for years known for its innovation capabilities, before it was taken over by a bigger natural resources group Rio Tinto, was the British company Borax. Borax, was in the business of mining boron. In many ways it was a mining company like many others, except it specialized in boron. It was also quite different from its peer mining companies, in that boron applications were not as numerous and did not require as great volumes as was the case with some other metals like bauxite (alumina) and ferrous metals in general. The innovation that marked Borax from its competitors and ensured its longevity, was the creation of an internal unit that looked for new applications for boron. In effect, Borax had the boron ore and it needed the applications to drive the volume. Instead of waiting for the market alone to come up with new applications, Borax decided to lend the market a hand by identifying new applications and educating the market about them. So, Borax reinvented what a specialist mining company could do and innovated volume for its mines itself.

The four rather different examples of innovation outlined above (i.e. new pharmaceutical compounds, new menu items in food retailing, patents not directly relevant to a company's own products, new applications for a mining company's main mineral product) and the contrasting nature of companies engaged in them, show that the relevance of innovation to a company's own products, own customer and own markets, is an important marker and determinant of the contribution innovation can make to a company's prospects of longevity.

It is therefore the duty of a Board of Directors to not only encourage investment in research and development or innovation in the broader sense, but to also ensure such innovation is indeed relevant to the company itself and its customers and markets. In this context, a Board needs to consider the short-, medium- and long-term consequences of investment in innovation. Moreover, seeking ways to embed innovation in the DNA of the company is potentially one of the most important responsibilities of a Board.

Three final and important case studies demonstrate the rewards afforded to companies with innovation in their DNA and the costs associated with the absence of innovation, lapse in embracing it continuously or complacency in the face of competitors' technological advances.

Everyone is familiar with Apple and its founder Steve Jobs continues to be revered years after his death. But it is worth noting that Steve Jobs, who had founded Apple in 1977, had been ousted from all his positions in Apple in 1985, by none other than John Sculley, the CEO he had himself recruited after five months of courtship from his position as CEO of Pepsi with the legendary pitch "Do you want to sell sugared water the rest of your life? Or do you want to come with me and change the world?" At the time Apple's computers were widely acknowledged and acclaimed for their capabilities, clever operating system and cool design but Apple was trailing in terms of the mass volume achieved by the personal computer (PC) made by IBM and other companies, with its then less acclaimed Microsoft operating system. Jobs felt that Sculley, a successful manager with PepsiCo Inc, could strengthen Apple's capabilities in a two-horse race between the PC and Apple's computers, similar to the one Coca-Cola and PepsiCo were fighting to their mutual benefit for decades. He offered Sculley the CEO position and initially Apple did benefit from his considerable marketing nous. But, as Jobs continued to yield unchecked power inside the division he led, a power struggle ensued when Sculley attempted to stamp his authority as CEO. In the battle between the seasoned and successful manager with excellent marketing credentials and the charismatic technology innovator whose winning touch seemed to have abandoned him with the less than stellar results of the Lisa computer, the Apple Board chose the manager. Whilst Sculley did have a few good years and some successes as Apple's CEO, by 1993 Apple was falling behind and in need of a turnaround and was himself turfed out by the Apple Board. Three years later, with Apple still in need of a turnaround, Steve Jobs, who had rehabilitated his reputation as a successful and visionary innovator with Pixar, the movie studio, was invited back.

The second coming of Steve Jobs culminated in innovation after innovation of whole categories of new and innovative products. First the iPod, then the iPhone, then the iPad and in parallel the revamping of the Mac computer range. Today, Apple is the most valuable company in the world and Apple is synonymous with design and innovation.

And yet, Apple was not the first company to make a big name for itself in mobile phones. Motorola from the US and Ericsson from Sweden were important competitors in the pre-Apple era. This was not surprising as both had long been associated with telecommunications electronics. But the company that dominated the mobile phone market before Apple was Nokia, a Finnish company, which had started as a rubber boots manufacturer in 1865. Multiple transformations later, Nokia became a force in mobile handsets in the early 1990s and by 2007, half of all mobile phones sold globally were made by Nokia, and its Symbian mobile phone operating system commanded 65% market share. Much of its success in the mobile phone market was credited to the foresight and leadership of Jorma Ollila, its CEO from 1992 to 2006, who divested all other divisions and focused the company on mobile phones. It was a decision that recognized both the potential of the mobile phone market and the historical connection of Nokia to it via its involvement in the development of the GSM standard in telecommunications in the 1980s. Under Ollila's leadership, Nokia became synonymous with innovation and design. For more than a decade, Nokia maintained its leading market position with enviable margins and market share. Its iconic banana shape mobile phone handset was a global hit. Suddenly and for a while, Finland, a country of 5.5 million people, became almost synonymous with Nokia. Ollila's transformation of Nokia became the subject of case studies for business schools around the world. Then Research In Motion appeared on the scene with a smartphone they called the BlackBerry and Nokia was too slow to recognize that this was a new wave that they needed to ride. The advantages of market leadership when competing against the likes of Motorola and Ericsson who were essentially selling the same telecoms product as Nokia with marginal differentiation on design, became crippling switching costs when competing against Research In Motion which was reinventing the mobile phone and with their BlackBerry were offering a computer with voice communication capabilities instead of a pure telecoms device. Soon after the introduction of the BlackBerry, Apple joined the market with their version of the smartphone, the iPhone.

Nokia was slow to recognize and respond to the smartphone revolution and BlackBerry very quickly became the preferred mobile phone of business users. Research in Motion and its two co-CEOs became lauded for their BlackBerry which continued to appeal to business users with its keyboard and email features. Meanwhile, Apple was adopting its own smartphone to deliver a bigger screen and a keyboard via a touch screen.

As Apple continued to innovate and enhance the capabilities of successive generations of the iPhone, Nokia fell from its pedestal and fell behind in the overall market and so did Research In Motion in the business segment of the market. Nokia's response was to partner with Microsoft and eventually to exit the mobile phone handset business. Its market capitalization which had peaked at $250 billion in 2000, went from $153 billion in 2007 down to $6 billion in 2012. For the company that underwent multiple transformations since its foundation in 1865, it was time for yet another transformation. After repositioning itself in the telecoms hardware and software business, Nokia's market capitalization recovered to $37 billion by 2017 and today is still a respectable $ 24 billion, but far from its glory days.

The company and its management, which had been hailed for being brave enough to ride the first wave of mobile phones, missed the boat of the smartphone revolution. Yet, through embracing transformational change one more time, the company has continued to exist, albeit with vastly different workforce, management and leadership. Indeed, from 2012 to early 2017, Nokia turned over 99% of the employee base, 80% of the Board and all but one member of the executive team.

Research In Motion's fall from grace was even more permanent than Nokia's. Having renamed itself BlackBerry and having tried and failed to match Apple's innovative smartphones, it retreated to much lower volumes and more niche segments with a market capitalization that was less than 10% of its heyday.

1.3.9.1.c. Historical Market Capitalization Apple, Nokia, Research in Motion

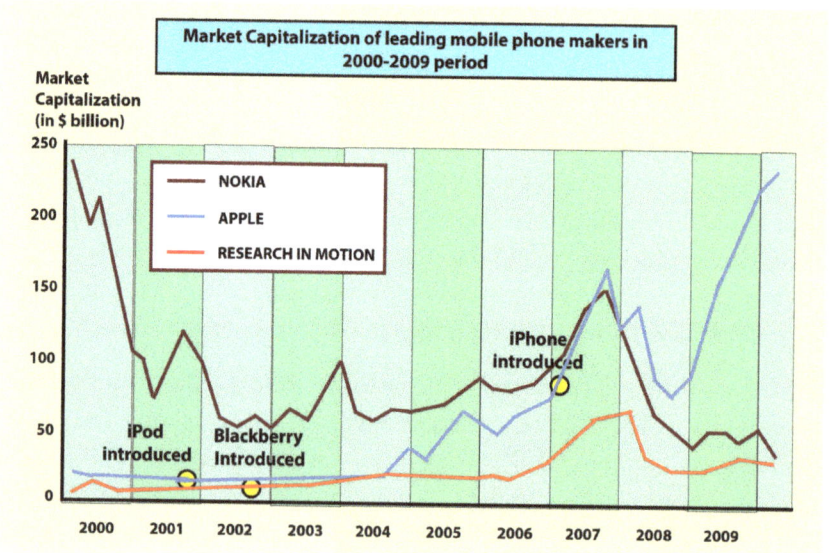

The experiences of Apple, Nokia and Research In Motion are instructive. Innovation can make a company's fortunes but it requires courage at Board and management level. Moreover, in sectors with high technological content, sustaining success requires sustained innovation. You can ride an innovation wave to the top but you won't stay at the top for long if you are not prepared to keep innovating. And if you have the resources, then it's better you do the innovating that you fear from your competition yourself rather than wrest on your laurels and risk letting challengers hurting you with their innovation. In this context, a Board has a responsibility to seek to embed innovation in the culture and DNA of the company.

1.3.9.2. Link of frequency and level of strategy review to sector

We have already encountered and discussed the need for a Board of Directors to review the strategy of their company once a year and the materials that can help inform such review and discussion. For example, we discussed the SWOT and PESTEL analytical tools and their use in informing Board reviews and discussions on strategy. But, is an annual review at the Board level enough? Or should there be other discussions and reviews at different levels of a company? And is there a link between how the discipline of strategic reviews take place and the sector of the company?

In answering these questions, it is helpful to remember the different nature of the strategic choices companies face in different sectors. For retailers, there is nothing more strategic than determining what is the product mix on offer to consumer in the stores and increasingly over the internet. For natural resource companies, capital investment decisions concerning exploration, extraction and processing are critically strategic as they set the direction of the companies for many years. As we have already seen, technology companies selling to consumers like Apple and Nokia need to identify and ride technological innovation waves and preferably engineer them themselves, if they wish to maintain their market position.

Let us now consider the example of a chain of convenient stores. How would questions of product mix be analyzed and determined? Unsurprisingly, by monitoring the actual sales and identifying trends. Or let us consider how the most successful of restaurant chains, McDonald's, remains a Dow Jones component by looking at how the product mix of the ubiquitous McDonald's had evolved over time and the local menu items you find in McDonald's around the world, along with the ubiquitous hamburger, intended to cater to local tastes – for example the spinach-pie in McDonald's in Greece and the beer in Belgium. Responsiveness to customer needs and preferences is clearly understood as being very important in certain sectors like fast-moving consumer goods (FMCG) and retailing, in order to maintain the connection with the end-customer. In such sectors innovation is easily copied and once a trend is visible, multiple players join it and accelerate it. Being nimble and identifying a trend first can provide very significant advantage but does not guarantee success if investment is timid or execution is flawed, because followers can catch-up and overtake the early innovators.

Let us also consider the example of extractive industries, like mining and energy. Technological innovation is fairly limited and capital investments in new production or processing facilities take years to be completed and are expected to last and deliver their returns over decades. Yet, even in these industries, there are technological advances that can impact demand and supply. New usages for certain materials can increase demand and create scarcity conditions and values, which may last or be transient. For example, when nuclear power seemed to be the answer to ever-growing energy needs and nuclear plants were considered sufficiently safe, uranium mining companies were attracting a great deal of investor interest and commanded hefty valuations. But things changed after the Fukushima disaster and as some major economies like Germany turned their back on nuclear plants, the anticipated increases in demand did not materialize. Currently, there is a great deal of excitement about lithium batteries as electrification of road transportation seems the accepted prospective technology that could overtake the internal combustion engine as the world tries to limit emissions. It remains to be seen if the investments in new lithium mining and processing facilities will indeed pay off for their investors or whether yet newer technologies like fuel cells will steal the thunder of lithium. The same concerns for the climate and the environment have also meant that practically all the oil majors have changed their traditional focus on oil and gas and have made and continue to make significant investments in renewable energy sources as they seek to transform themselves into broader energy companies.

The examples above suggest that the frequency of the strategy review needs to take into account the nature of the industry. Clearly such awareness is important for a Board and a management team. But there are also proactive measures a Board and a management team can take to ensure innovation and strategic reviews are afforded the attention they deserve. Given that all business activity is competitive and Boards and management teams aim to keep their businesses at or near the top for as long as possible, it is useful to at least consider the world of competitive sport. In competitive sport, the recognition of who is best is tied with moments in time by having calendars of sporting events. In many sports, success at the Olympics is the pinnacle of achievement. In other sports it's World Cups that are considered the pinnacle. In most sports, these events tend to take place every four years. In politics, four- or five-year cycles are also the most usual periods when votes are asked to extend existing mandates or grant new ones.

Is there value in companies also subjecting themselves in some form of introspection and forward thinking every few years? The author believes that by formalizing a periodic strategy review across a company's organization with staff encouraged to submit ideas and engage in open debate, a Board signals that strategy and change is not the preserve of management and the Board. It can also provide an opportunity for the company's employees to put forward both evolutionary and revolutionary ideas concerning their areas. During such periodic and company-wide reviews, employees can be given license to challenge the old "We have always done it this way" with the question "Should we carry on doing it this way for another X years, or is there a better way?"

1.3.10. Culture

1.3.10.1. What is Culture in the context of Corporate Governance?

The culture of organizations has been studied extensively and there are entire books written on the subject. The purpose of this subchapter is not to expand on organizational or company culture in general but to examine the role Culture can play specifically in the context of Corporate Governance.

Company Culture is often defined as the shared values, attributes, expectations and practices the characterize the actions of and interactions of company members between themselves and with external parties. It is also often defined to include attitudes and behaviours since these are of course linked to the values members of a company, be they employees, management or directors, hold. If companies could be considered as exhibiting a human personality through the actions of their employees, management and directors, then a company's Culture would be the company's personality. It is clear from the definition that every company has its own culture which is shaped by the people in the company and which in turn also influences their behaviour and actions. First of all, a company with a strongly discernible culture will tend to attract people who are comfortable with that culture. This will tend to reinforce the prevailing culture. Secondly, observable behaviour at all levels of a company in different circumstances set the tone and expectations for all employees in a much more direct way than policy documents and staff manuals.

So, Culture has reflexive and transmission qualities. It is these reflexive and transmission qualities of Culture that are most relevant to Corporate Governance.

1.3.10.2. How and why does Culture matter?

Given its reflexive and transmission qualities the type of culture a company exhibits matters a great deal when it comes to Corporate Governance. Certain ingredients in a company culture promote Corporate Governance such as:

✓ Integrity – the quality of being honest and having strong moral principles is entirely in keeping with good Corporate Governance and employees in companies with cultures which include integrity as a key ingredient are much more likely to adhere to their companies' Code of Conduct and generally stay within boundaries laid out by the principles of good Corporate Governance

✓ Trust – being able to rely on one's colleagues and management in sharing information and working through issues, problems, challenges and crises, creates predictable patterns of behaviour in normal times as well as resilient reactions to changes in circumstances. This is also in keeping with good Corporate Governance

✓ Transparency and accountability – these twins are crucial in ensuring an environment where checks and balances are understood as crucial for the longevity of the company and in this respect are entirely supportive of good Corporate Governance.

✓ Demonstrable commitment to values – as actions speak much louder than words and documents, the behaviours of a company's leaders and managers need to be demonstrably aligned with the values the company identifies as its own. Leading by setting a good example is certainly supportive of good Corporate Governance. Similarly, reacting quickly and decisively to aberrant behaviour that questions or undermines the values of the company can be equally powerful in terms of culture and in terms of promoting Corporate Governance.

Characteristics of a company culture that can undermine Corporate Governance include:

➢ Moral ambiguity – absence of clear moral principles and moral ambiguity make it very difficult for employees to rely on a common moral compass in their dealings on behalf of the company and with each other. In environments with such elements in the culture, Corporate Governance will suffer and inevitably some employees and managers will stray, potentially with serious consequences. Bribery and corruption are just two examples that spring to mind as examples of behaviour into which employees can stray into when moral ambiguity characterizes a company's culture.

➢ Unchecked concentration of power – notwithstanding charismatic leaders and entrepreneurs who build successful businesses, the unchecked concentration of power and its exercise by a single individual or a small coterie around a paramount type leader, breeds all manner of risks and is generally quite inconsistent with the checks and balances approach which good Corporate Governance exemplifies. This is not to assume that all leaders who have such unchecked power will abuse it, but simply to state the rather obvious fact that it is far easier for such leaders to abuse their power than where power is more widely distributed.

➤ Win at all costs attitudes – though on occasion win at all costs attitudes may be facilitated by moral ambiguity we have encountered already, such attitudes can stay entirely within the rule of law and still be inconsistent with good Corporate Governance. This is because win at all costs attitudes inevitably lead to compromising and even betraying values and principles and without values and principles there is no Corporate Governance.

➤ Arrogance – very few individual senior managers would ever admit to being consciously arrogant or knowingly behaving arrogantly, but long periods of corporate success can sometimes breed feelings and more dangerously still, conviction, in groups of senior executives that they know better than others, including customers, suppliers and regulators and that normal rules do not apply to them. When such feelings or convictions begin to take hold in an organization, the arrogant behaviour that often follows, can corrode any principles of Corporate Governance if managers make the mistake of thinking that checks and balances are relevant to others but not to them.

Ultimately, culture can play a catalytic role in what type of Corporate Governance is actually practiced as opposed to what the relevant Code of Conduct and even regulations prescribe. It is therefore incumbent on a Board and a management team who wish to promote good Corporate Governance to ensure that their company's culture at a minimum, promotes integrity, trust, transparency and accountability.

1.3.10.3. How do you promote and harness culture in the context of Corporate Governance?

The most important way for companies to promote culture in a way that is supportive of good Corporate Governance is through the actions of its leaders, including its directors and its executive management team all the way to line managers. Employees are quick to notice any misalignment between what behaviour is prescribed for them and what is being practiced by the management or the Board. Harnessing culture in promotion of Corporate Governance requires vigilance, self-discipline and integrity on the part of the Board and the management.

Another important way companies can achieve a desired culture that promotes Corporate Governance is to be mindful of cultural fit when they recruit new employees. Rigorous selection processes which allow a candidate to really appreciate a company's culture and for the recruiters to assess the potential cultural fit, may appear more costly than less rigorous approaches but the benefits of cultural fit for new recruits cannot be underestimated once a company actually has the culture it wishes to maintain. Recruits who are taken on without proper assessment and then found out to be unable to fit in, create significant extra costs as they inevitably increase employee turnover and valuable time and resources are wasted.

Of course, staff manuals, induction courses and other training courses as well as other corporate events play an important role in transmitting commitment to a particular culture, which hopefully is supportive of Corporate Governance. Company communications, including through social media and company websites also are transmission mechanisms that signal to the world at large as well as the employees of a company what the company's culture is and the level of its commitment to Corporate Governance.

In the end, culture can indeed promote or undermine Corporate Governance, depending on how leaders and managers signal their commitment to Corporate Governance and how they confirm such commitment through their actions. For good or bad, employees tend to follow leaders' examples not policy documents as actions speak louder than words and are remembered for far longer.

1.4. Chapter closing thoughts

Good Corporate Governance requires much more than mere adherence to prescribed codes. It requires ongoing attention to all its ingredients and building blocks we have examined in this chapter as well as the active promotion of an appropriate culture of transparency, accountability and respect to the principle and practice of checks and balances. As we will see in the next chapter, inattention to these matters does not bode well for companies.

Chapter 2:
Failures of Corporate Governance

2.1. The impact of poor Corporate Governance on a company

Corporate Governance cannot completely compensate for a poor business model or an uncompetitive product or market position or technological obsolescence. But effective Corporate Governance should at least correctly identify opportunities, challenges and risks and provide room for rational decision-making and adjustments to be made where the survival of a business is at stake. Even so, good Corporate Governance practices are not a guarantee against business underperformance or even failure. Instead, good Corporate Governance can be likened to a safety valve mechanism that at the very least can prevent catastrophic and sudden failure. In contrast, poor or non-existent Corporate Governance is corrosive and can lead not only to underperformance but also spectacular, precipitous and catastrophic business failure. So, whereas good Corporate Governance is not associated with dramatic changes in business fortunes, dramatic declines in business fortunes are often understood after the fact as being linked to poor or non-existent Corporate Governance that preceded such declines or failures.

In order to consider examples of poor Corporate Governance, one can look to the definitions we have encountered already and examine if some or all of the ingredients for Corporate Governance have been present, absent or compromised. In simple terms, how and where have the checks and balances been affecting the business. For example:

- ✓ Is the Board effective in how it acts as a check on the activities of the management?
- ✓ Does the management act in a way that ensures the business is adequately protected from excessive risk taking in whatever form?
- ✓ Are appropriate checks and balances prevalent and respected within

the business in respect of activities which create material risk exposures to the business?

✓ Is there a culture that promotes openness, accountability and respect of laws and regulations or a culture of secrecy and testing legal and regulatory boundaries?

Some examples of Corporate Governance failures can be quite instructive as illustrated below:

2.1.1.   The Barings Bank collapse example – Special rules for a star trader

Barings Bank, a venerable privately-held bank in the City of London, had a history of over 200 years when it collapsed over a weekend in 1995. It had weathered the ups and downs of the British economy and two World Wars and was considered a rather solid bank when it emerged that its capital base had been irretrievably holed by the trading of a single individual in its Singapore branch. Overnight, or so it seemed, the bank was gone.

What had gone wrong? As the facts emerged, it became clear that the risk-taking of one individual trader, Nick Leeson, had somehow been allowed to escalate to the point where he was in effect betting the bank. It turned out that Leeson's initially profitable trading had encouraged senior management to let him have bigger positions and subsequently to essentially act as his own back office in processing, controlling, monitoring and reporting his trading. When his trading was not as profitable as he would like or was loss making, he was in a position to mask this and the senior management in London was none the wiser – until the scale of his positions and his associated losses became so big, he could not hide this any longer. Cue criminal prosecution and jail time for Nick Leeson, followed by the obligatory book and movie telling the story from his perspective – though both appropriately named *Rogue Trader* – to allow him to pay something back to those who lost so much from the collapse.

Whilst Nick Leeson obviously bore the personal responsibility for his actions, they would not have been possible and their disastrous consequences would have been avoided if the simple rule that "No trader can act as his own back office" had been maintained. It was not as if Barings did not know of this simple rule or that it had not been observing it with respect to other traders.

They did know the value of the rule and its importance. Their decision to relax this rule for their "star" trader was a manifestation of poor Corporate Governance, that had a disastrous impact on the whole bank.

The financial services industry is littered with examples of star traders or teams which have cost their respective institutions very substantial sums and sometimes even their independence as a firm.

For example, consider the following:

> Joseph Jett at Kidder Peabody in 1994 – who ran the investment bank's government bond trading desk and having found an accounting glitch relating to STRIPS (Separate Trading of Registered Interest and Principal Securities, essentially government bonds without their coupons) did not report it but used it to show profits when his trades were in fact loss-making. Senior management were happy to reward their star trader who over a short three years in charge of the desk had generated ~$350 million in profits, without ever questioning anything. But, the trick to his profits was to roll positions forward rather than close them and thus in order to keep booking profits, he ended up needing more and more false trades. When he was eventually discovered, he was supposed to have made trades worth $1.76 trillion of which only $79 billion were real and the accumulated profits of ~$350 million, turned out to be losses of ~$85 million. General Electric, the then the owner of Kidder Peabody, sold its stake to Paine Webber in the aftermath of the scandal. Jett was fined $8 million by the Securities and Exchange Commission.

> Jérôme Kerviel – at Société Générale in early 2008 – who took massive directional positions vastly exceeding his authorized limits with the closing of these positions costing Société Générale ~€4.9 billion in losses in January 2008. Though Kerviel claimed to have generated profits of €2 billion for Société Générale to the end of 2007, he was accused, convicted and jailed for three years for fraud, breach of trust and forgery. However, in 2016, he also won a claim against Société Générale for unfair dismissal with one of the tribunal's judges noting that the bank could not pretend it was unaware of his fake operations.

Of course in all these cases the traders and very often their superiors lost their jobs and often the traders themselves also faced prosecution. But the other common theme that emerges is how often reported profits can confer "star" status and create compliance gaps that the "star" traders can use to their advantage, and how often management prefers to book the profits without questions rather than scrutinize and risk losing their "star" trader to one of their competitors.

The spread of this phenomenon across different banks and jurisdictions, despite all of the banks concerned being familiar with Corporate Governance and its building blocks, also raises the question of what may have been missing that allowed such "star" traders to turn rogue. One very plausible explanation is that trading environments with great emphasis on risk taking, with most praise, reward and status being afforded to those delivering the biggest profits, whilst back-office and compliance functions are perceived as acting as a handbrake and red tape, are areas where Corporate Governance is not part of the culture and whatever culture of Corporate Governance does permeate the organization is not as genuine and ingrained as it should be.

2.1.2. The Polly Peck example – No real checks by a Board of a listed company on a founder CEO

Polly Peck was a darling of the London stock exchange in the 1980s. From humble beginnings, it had become a constituent of the FTSE100 index. Its fall from grace in 1990 was spectacular and was accompanied by the arrest of its founder CEO Asil Nadir, his fleeing in 1993 beyond the reach of British justice and a delayed trial and conviction of the CEO years later (2012) for theft. How did a CEO with an apparent Midas touch who took Polly Peck from its humble origins into a powerhouse of fruit and vegetable trading, end up in the dock and in jail with thousands of shareholders and creditors millions out of pocket? It transpired that Asil Nadir had trouble distinguishing between personal and company property and his Board of Directors was not sufficiently strong to keep him in check. So, whilst the company prospered, he extracted value by transferring funds to offshore accounts without the knowledge of the Board and when the company's fortunes turned, and the auditors spotted the transfers and the Board requested corrective actions, he was unwilling or unable to reverse the flows. Along with the collapse of the Bank of Credit and Commerce International (BCCI) in the early 1990s which exhibited similar shortcomings of poor Corporate Governance also linked to an all-powerful CEO with ability to act as he pleased, the Polly Peck collapse prompted the UK authorities to appoint the Cadbury commission which resulted in the Cadbury Report on Corporate Governance in 1991–92. Not surprisingly, a key recommendation from the Cadbury Commission was the splitting of the Chairman and CEO roles and the appointment of two persons to fulfil the roles so that no one person could ever accumulate and potentially abuse such powers as Asil Nadir had done.

Examples of weak or compliant Boards abound in multiple industries and when combined with incompetence or worse still dishonesty at the management level, it is of course a recipe for disaster. Sometimes, the cost is borne by the shareholders of the companies concerned but in the financial sector, they can cause ripples far and wide and sometimes take whole countries down with them. For example, think of and look up the following:

> The story of Marfin Popular Bank in Cyprus – excessive risk taking with oversize exposure to Greek government bonds during the Greek financial crisis, aggressive international expansion and excessive concentration of risk in its loan portfolio, all with the apparent knowledge of a compliant Board which included directors who were themselves or their companies heavily indebted to the bank, left it in need of recapitalization in 2011 after the European Council's decision for the private sector participation in the bailing out of Greece (i.e. the haircut imposed on the holders of Greek government bonds) that led to its nationalization and then collapse in 2013

> Royal Bank of Scotland – excessive empire building by a CEO unchecked by a Board that was found lacking in backbone, that led to one last expensive acquisition too many (ABN AMRO) at the top of the cycle which left the bank in need of recapitalization during the 2008 financial crisis and led to its state-led rescue and part nationalization in 2008

> Enron – failures of Corporate Governance at many levels with the story made into a gripping and eye-opening documentary called, perhaps ironically, *The Smartest Guys in the Room*.

One common denominator in most of the cases mentioned as examples in this section was the presence of a strong culture that was incompatible with the very notion of checks and balances which is at the heart of Corporate

Governance and which added extra wind to the sails of leaders who were willing to sail dangerously close to rocky shores. Convinced of their own exceptionalism, the leaders of these organizations may have paid lip-service to Corporate Governance and may have ticked a lot of its boxes but they never promoted a culture of Corporate Governance.

2.2. Impact of failure or financial distress of a company's counterparty

Poor Corporate Governance can lead to a company experiencing financial distress and possibly failing. This is true not only for a company itself but also for all its counterparties. And if any of the company's counterparties experience financial distress or worse, fail, the company itself is also impacted. As the diagram below illustrates the impact from failure or financial distress of its counterparties can affect a company in a number of different ways, depending of course on what type of counterparty is involved.

Figure 2.2.a. Impact of financial distress on counterparties

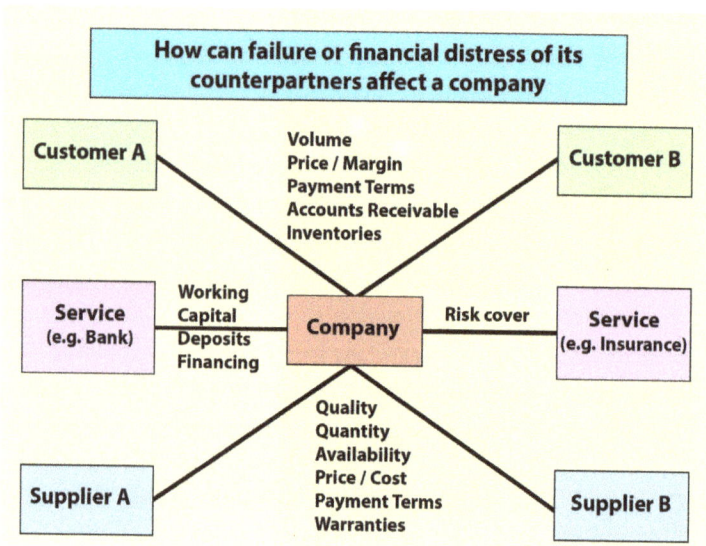

How can failure/financial distress in a supplier affect a company?

Failure or financial distress in a supplier can lead to declining or unacceptable quality of the goods being delivered to the company. There could also be shortages or unpredictability in terms of delivered volumes. Any of the above can have a short-term negative impact on the company's own production, at least until the company secures alternative sources of supply. There could also be financial costs from the negative impact on the company's own production, or advance payments that may never be recovered or warranty claims that prove uncollectable. Another potential pitfall from a supplier's failure or financial distress are the higher prices and more demanding payment terms that may become the norm afterwards, either from the supplier in distress (for example earlier prices might have been artificially low and payment terms overly generous) or new suppliers the company tries to replace them with. Given the disruption supplier failures can cause, it is not surprising that as part of prudent Risk Management, most companies try hard to avoid overreliance on a single source of supply for critical inputs.

How can failure or financial distress in a client affect a company?

Failure or financial distress in a client can lead to declining or unpredictable demand for the company's goods or services. Beyond such a negative effect on sales, there can also be negative impact on prices, margins and cashflow. There could be uncertainty over the ability of the impacted client to honour payment terms which could lead the company to insist on cash sales which in turn could have a negative effect on volume of sales. Uncertainty can also impact the recoverability of accounts receivable on sales already made and recognized in the company's accounts. Reduced demand and sales from the impacted client would mean the company needing to find alternative clients for its products or services. Another element of the company's balance sheet to be affected could be the value of the inventory in light of uncertainty of demand, especially if such inventory was customized to requirements of the client experiencing financial distress or failing. And beyond accounting for it on the balance sheet, financing costs of inventory, both of finished goods and raw materials, could create a double whammy, to the extent products were customized to the particular client's requirements and finding new clients with the same requirements proves difficult. Given the severe impact a client's financial distress can have on a company, it is not surprising that most companies try very hard to diversify their sales and avoid becoming overreliant on any individual clients.

How can failure or financial distress of a banking services provider affect a company?

Banks rarely fail but when they do, their creditors can be severely impacted. Thus, a company with significant cash balances in a bank that fails, may find itself losing deposits beyond the particular jurisdiction's insured level and thus suffering a direct cash hit. Depending on whether the company has other deposits with other banks and accounts receivable that can be quickly collected, such a direct cash hit could impact liquidity to such a degree that the company experiences knock-on effect on operations and competitive market position. Bank failures can also lead to higher costs for banking services as the impacted company establishes new banking relationships with a new bank. Given the potentially very negative impact of a bank's failure on a client company, it is not surprising that the old adage of not putting all your eggs in one basket is both the guiding principle that encourages companies to have multiple banking relationships and a mark of disciplined Risk Management as part of good Corporate Governance.

How can failure or financial distress of an insurance provider affect a company?

Insurers, similar to banks, also rarely fail or experience financial distress, but when they do their clients can be severely impacted. Potential loss of premium already paid is an obvious negative impact. Another is the potential loss of desired insurance cover if no other insurer is providing exactly the same cover. A further potential negative impact are potentially higher costs for same or similar cover going forward, particularly if the earlier low pricing is deemed unsustainable by a new insurance provider.

2.3. Red flags and lessons from Corporate Governance Failures

Whilst there are many case studies written and taught on companies which failed and where failures in Corporate Governance contributed to the financial distress and ultimate failure of the companies concerned, a common characteristic of many of these cases is that until the final few days or weeks, more often than not, these companies were considered sound and in many cases quite successful. For example, Lehman Brothers went from being one of the most admired and profitable investment banks in 2007 to bankrupt in 2008. Similarly, WorldCom, Enron and Waste Management were perceived as market leaders in their respective industries before they were laid low by accounting scandals. Their fall from grace was as quick and precipitous as it was spectacular. Where were the red flags that could have alerted clients, investors, regulators on the impending difficulties? The answer is complex and must factor in the role that the external auditors played and the extent to which criminality may have been involved.

2.3.1. Red flags and lessons from industrial companies' failures.

In seeking to draw lessons from company failures it is instructive to look at high profile cases which have attracted significant coverage in the press as well as scrutiny by relevant regulatory or even law enforcement authorities. The information that becomes publicly available as a result allows lessons to be drawn based on commonly accepted facts and chronologies rather than subjective interpretations of limited data. The level of information that becomes available in such high-profile cases is also useful in trying to identify red flags that could have alerted interested parties of the troubles ahead. In this context, we look at four high profile failures in Corporate Governance, two of which also led to the collapse of the companies concerned.

2.3.1.1. Waste Management – accounting irregularities

In the 1999 case of Waste Management – a leading company in the waste management industry, which had grown both organically and through many acquisitions – the founder and CEO along with a small group of senior executives engineered increased earnings by lengthening the depreciation period on plant and equipment as well as understating expenses and thereby artificially inflating earnings, with the connivance of external auditors (Arthur Andersen) who acquiesced when promised additional fees and signed off the company's statements when they should have rejected the founder CEO's use of inappropriate accounting policies and practices. When a new CEO and management team found out and came clean, the company restated its earnings to the tune of $1.7 billion, then the largest restatement in history and the company's share price inevitably took a very big hit. But the company survived and eventually the share price recovered and climbed further. It obviously helped that the balance sheet was still sound and that it was the company's own senior management acknowledging the problems and putting their house in order. It is clear that the external auditors caught the fraud but opted to go along with it and for this they were fined $7 million by the relevant regulator. But were there any flags that could have alerted investors of the cosiness of the external auditors with the founder CEO and his senior management team? It turns out the company's CFO had trained as an auditor with Arthur Andersen and the company's Chief Administrative Officer had been a 30-year veteran and partner in Arthur Andersen and in fact had been the partner in charge of the Waste Management account before joining Waste Management. The company's VP Finance was also an Arthur Andersen alumnus who had been audit manager for Waste Management. So, in addition to potentially benchmarking the company's accounting policies with their competitors' policies (e.g. comparing their respective depreciation period policies), the most important flag was indeed the very cosy relationship between the external auditors and the company manifesting itself with three executives in key finance positions.

2.3.1.2. Enron – 2001 collapse

In the case of Enron, a market leading and politically well-connected energy trading company, analysts were gushing in their praise of the company's profitability and pioneering ways which were seen as redefining the energy trading industry. Suspicions were raised when Jeffrey Skilling resigned as CEO in August 2001 after less than a year in the job, citing personal reasons and selling large amounts of stock shortly thereafter. The company collapsed in December 2001. It turned out that fraudulent accounting by a clique of insiders had been flattering the company's financial performance and condition by keeping debts off the balance sheet and in ways that enriched certain insiders. The performance that had looked to be redefining an industry was a mirage and in fact too good to be true. The external auditors, Arthur Andersen again, had been negligent and did not survive the scandal. Skilling and other key senior managers faced congressional hearings and eventually served long periods of jail time for their role in the fraud. The short seller who first bet against Enron, the Greek American Jim Chanos of Kynikos Associates (Kynikos means cynic in Greek) established himself as a short seller whose positions became worthy of checking and considering as at least amber flags. In Enron's case there were at least two flags to raise the alarm and prompt questions: Skilling's resignation and off-loading of Enron stock as well as the short selling by Chanos.

2.3.1.3. WorldCom - collapse

Another very high-profile collapse was that of WorldCom in 2002. At the time, WorldCom was the second largest long distance telecoms operator in the US. The company had grown rapidly via acquisitions, often using its shares as acquisition currency under its buccaneering CEO Bernie Ebbers. It turned out that from 1999 to 2002, senior executives at WorldCom had inflated assets, underreported costs by capitalizing expenses and inflated revenues by fake accounting entries. They were found out by the company's internal audit in June 2002 who estimated $3.8 billion of fraudulent balance sheet entries. By that time the company's stock had already lost 94% of its value due to SEC investigations that had started earlier that year and concerns over the $30 billion mountain of debt the company was carrying. Eventually, WorldCom was forced to admit that it had overstated its assets by over $11 billion. At the time, it was the largest accounting fraud in American history. The internal auditor who unearthed the fraud, Cynthia Cooper, had in effect acted as a whistleblower, whilst the CEO who orchestrated the fraud to inflate earnings and thus support the company's stock price, ended up serving a 14-year jail sentence. Interestingly, Cynthia Cooper had prioritized the specific internal audit following press coverage of concerns expressed by a former accounting employee of WorldCom who had been laid off in March 2001. In this case the flags included the use of stock as acquisition currency which created a strong incentive for senior WorldCom executives to find ways to keep their stock price high.

The scandals of Enron and WorldCom led to the introduction of Sarbanes–Oxley legislation. The Act, often referred as SOX, creates, among other elements, specific responsibility on the CEO and CFO for financial reporting as well as the internal control system of their companies and criminalizes certification of misleading or fraudulent financial statements. It also established whistleblower job protection.

2.3.1.4. Tesco – accounting irregularity

In the UK, size and reputation have also proved to be no guarantee against Corporate Governance failure. In 2014, Tesco, the country's largest retailer and third largest globally, was enmeshed in an accounting irregularity scandal when it transpired that it had overinflated revenues and profits by recognizing rebates from suppliers as revenues prior to the sales of the goods involved. Though at £263 million the irregularity was material, the size and strength of Tesco's balance sheet meant it weathered the inevitable storm. It turned out that the external auditors had flagged recognition of income from rebates was at risk of manipulation but the Board Audit Committee did not challenge Tesco's executive management who were manipulating the accounts in order to cover slowing performance and meet margin targets. When the scandal broke, four senior executives, including the CFO, left with immediate effect and the company carried on without a full time CFO for two months as an external hire was recruited in light of the nature and scale of the irregularity. Perhaps the failure of the Audit Committee to respond to the concerns of the external auditors was the critical failure in Corporate Governance. And the red flag was the absence of non-executive directors at the Board level with relevant retailing experience.

2.3.1.5. Red flags in industrial companies

All in all, spotting red flags in industrial companies which could foretell future problems requires attention to practically all aspects of a company's operations, governance arrangements, ownership, culture, M&A activity, and more. The list below is illustrative and not an exhaustive checklist. It is intended to highlight the frame of mind one has to adopt and the nature of signals one has to become sensitive to, in order to recognize red flags in a timely fashion.

> ➤ Absence of commitment to Corporate Governance from the top – usually observable in the size and composition of a Board as well as

the frequency of its meetings and the existence or not and the staffing of important Board committees (e.g. Audit Committee)

➤ Culture of cutting corners and absence of controls. This could be evident in terms of marginal or no compliance on health and safety or environmental standards. Regulators' fines in these areas can be a useful signal to monitor. Such corner cutting could also be evident in loose documentation and variable standards. All interactions one has with a company can be observations and data points in gauging the company's culture

➤ Aggressive acquisitions particularly funded with shares if listed – companies growing on the back of large number of acquisitions in a short period do face integration challenges and if shares are used as acquisition currency, it could motivate management of the acquisitive company to use all means fair and foul to keep their share price high and thus their acquisition currency strong

➤ Boards without any non-executives or with non-executives with no real sectoral or other relevant experience as under these scenarios there will be no or little scrutiny of executive management

➤ High levels of borrowings and leverage, particularly if counter to the economic cycle, since this raises the risk of financial distress

➤ Low levels of liquidity and stretching payment terms

➤ Dominant shareholders mixing company with personal interests – this could include transactions involving the company's shares or assets which ordinarily must take place at arm's length

➤ Absence of or weak external and internal control mechanisms – for example no internal audit function and no external auditors or external auditors whose size appears mismatched to the complexity of the company

➤ Persistent under delivery vs. promised or contracted deliverables

➤ Quality issues with the company's products or services

➤ Deviations from industry or market norms in critical aspects of financial or operational performance – is there a credible explanation or reasoning or could it be too good to be true?

➤ Cosy relationships with external auditors – evident from lack of rotation of external auditing firms, lack of rotation of audit firm partner, past employment links

- ➢ Significant use of related parties in trading and in mergers and acquisitions (M&A) activity – trading or M&A activity with or through companies affiliated or controlled by key managers or shareholders present conflict of interest questions and could be the means by which managers or shareholders extract value from the business
- ➢ Frequent changes in external auditors, or CFO or Finance Director – as it could suggest unease on their part with what they are expected to sign off
- ➢ Underqualified external auditors for the size and complexity of the company – as size and complexity of a company increases, its audit becomes more demanding and therefore the relative standing and resources of the external auditors should generally match-up to their client companies' standing and resources
- ➢ In the case of listed companies, short positions can be important red flags, particularly if linked to short sellers questioning their target's business models and accounting practices – as short sellers have a strong incentive to explain to the rest of the market the validity of their position, they are usually quite prepared to share their analysis and reasoning behind their view of their target's prospects

Notwithstanding looking out for red flags, proactively managing risk arising from interactions with clients and suppliers is part of good Corporate Governance. In this context, companies and their Boards need to:

- ✓ Diversify intelligently – on the supply side in order to ensure security of supplies or avoid overreliance on single sourcing and on the demand side in order to avoid overreliance on one or a few clients
- ✓ Be aware of exposure levels to clients and suppliers and be prepared to make changes to ensure such exposure levels do not jeopardise the company's own standing in the event of distress or failure of clients or suppliers
- ✓ Actively gather and process information on clients and suppliers in order to spot early any trends or events that could create risks or pose threats to the company

2.3.2. Lessons and red flags from bank failures.

2.3.2.1. Lessons from bank failures

In Cyprus, Laiki Bank had been the challenger to its larger rival Bank of Cyprus for most of its existence. In 2006, a new shareholder, the Marfin Financial Group (MFG), acquired a 10% stake and was able to elect the bank's Board of Directors. At the time MFG had controlling stakes in two small Greek banks, Marfin Bank and Egnatia Bank and an investment banking subsidiary Investment Bank of Greece. Shortly thereafter, MFG engineered a reverse takeover of Laiki, whereby Laiki bought MFG by issuing Laiki shares to MFG's shareholders. The new group was still headquartered in Cyprus and was renamed Marfin Popular Bank and had a Greek subsidiary named Marfin Egnatia Bank. Following this merger, MFG raised €6 billion of capital from investors in a rights issue, in which Marfin Popular Bank did not participate and was renamed Marfin Investment Group (MIG). Nearly one-seventh of the capital raised from investors came from long term loans (some as long as 30–40 years) they were offered from Marfin Egnatia Bank with shares of MIG pledged as collateral. MIG proceeded to make a number of acquisitions in Greece and neighbouring countries with mixed results but always with financing readily available from Marfin Egnatia Bank or Marfin Popular Bank. In parallel, and on the back of bulging deposits in Cyprus, Marfin Popular Bank expanded internationally and into the markets of Serbia, Ukraine, Russia, Estonia and Malta whilst also aggressively expanding its loan portfolio in Greece and Cyprus. By early 2011, Marfin Popular Bank was almost the same size as its rival Bank of Cyprus and for some it was a matter of time before overtaking it. But, by late 2011, the Chairman and CEO of the bank had been forced out by the Cyprus Central Bank and in mid-2012 the bank was in effect nationalized (and reverted to its original Laiki name) when the Cyprus state underwrote a €1.8 billion recapitalization following massive losses the bank incurred as a result of its outsize exposure to Greek government bonds and the losses imposed on Greek government bondholders by Greece's European partners as a price for their continued support and solidarity. Then in March 2013, the bank, whose balance sheet was being propped up by €9 billion of Emergency Liquidity Assistance from the European Central Bank via the Cyprus Central Bank, was placed in resolution under the Cyprus Central Bank as part of the package of measures agreed between Cyprus and the TROIKA lenders (i.e. International

Monetary Fund, European Central Bank and European Union) and Cyprus's European partners.

The losses suffered by depositors (~$3.2 billion) and bondholders of Laiki (~$0.8 billion) were very significant for an island like Cyprus with a GDP of ~$17 billion in 2012. Understandably, various authorities undertook investigations, issued reports and levied fines on Laiki and some of its former executives. The picture that emerged from the investigations of the Cyprus Securities and Exchange Commission (CySEC) showed not only disproportionate exposure to Greek government bonds, but also aggressive lending including imprudently high related party lending, including to MIG and its investee companies and Board members of Laiki itself, coupled with lax provisioning. Up until its nationalization in mid-2012, the bank had been ticking all the boxes of Corporate Governance and had all the committees that its regulators expected. But the composition of the Board, as well as the lending to Board members and companies affiliated to them that was going on, had meant there was very little real scrutiny of the management by the Board. There were two sets of external auditors, Grant Thornton for the Greek operations and PWC for the Cypriot ones and the consolidation, who never qualified any of their opinions until the accounts for 2012, which as of writing are yet to be signed off.

What were the observable signals that could have alerted the regulators, the depositors and bondholders of what was to come? It turned out that the bank would engage in activities in Greece (e.g. lending money to clients to buy shares) that were prohibited in Cyprus as well as use the deposit base in Cyprus to expand the loan portfolio in Greece, in a kind of regulatory and jurisdiction arbitrage. Both regulators – the Bank of Greece and the Central Bank of Cyprus – had reservations about different aspects of the bank's policies but in the end neither took sufficient steps to curtail the excesses of these policies. The fact that Marfin Popular Bank's Chairman, Andreas Vgenopoulos, was an outspoken but charismatic Greek lawyer with political access, at least in Cyprus, who clashed occasionally with the Governor of the Cyprus Central Bank, could have been a red flag. Normally, bank regulators and senior bank executives do not spar in public. Reclassifications of Greek government bonds in 2009 and 2010 could have been another red flag, particularly when coming with a health warning that the reclassifications were reducing the losses that needed to be recognized otherwise. A further red flag could have been the very large related party lending that was going on. A lot of depositors did withdraw funds from the Greek or Cypriot branch of the bank, particularly after the private sector involvement (PSI) haircut of its Greek government bond holdings which resulted in a need for recapitalization. Indeed, increasing amounts of emergency liquidity assistance funding that was provided by the European Central Bank via the Cyprus Central Bank attests to a loss of depositor confidence which may have been linked with some of these signals or others. Still, when the bank collapsed, there were still very large numbers of depositors who found themselves as unsecured creditors of a bank in resolution and as of the time of writing more than nine years later are still waiting to receive whatever pennies on the dollar the liquidation of the Laiki estate will yield for them.

In the UK's version of the 2008 financial crisis, Northern Rock was the bank that succumbed to a literal run on the bank. In this case, the bank had the opposite problem from Laiki, in that where Laiki's surplus deposits had encouraged aggressive lending, investment and expansion that led to disaster, Norhern Rock had too few deposits relative to its loan portfolio and was reliant on wholesale funding to fund the expansion of its loan portfolio. When the 2008 financial crisis hit, the wholesale markets seized up as banks kept liquidity to themselves and Northern Rock found itself very quickly very short on liquidity and insolvent as collateral values also began to be affected. This lopsided reliance on wholesale markets may have been visible and understood by bank analysts and institutional players but not to the regular depositors. The Board of Northern Rock had simply not contemplated wholesale funding not being readily available and had liter-ally bet the existence of the bank on a business model which proved less robust and sustainable than they thought. It was a different kind of failure of governance than that encountered in Laiki above, but a failure none-theless, because if the Board does not ask the difficult "what if" questions, then who can help the management avoid relying on a wrong assumption or business model?

Whilst Laiki was a large fish in the relatively small pond of the Cyprus bank-ing sector and Northern Trust a relatively small fish in the much larger pond of the UK banking sector, the next example of financial distress concerned the American Insurance Group (AIG), one of the largest financial players in

107

the US financial markets, the largest in the world. AIG had many arms and was a leading player in insurance, asset management, securities lending (on the back of its asset management activities) as well as underwriting of credit default swaps (CDS). Indeed, when it came to CDSs – a form of insurance contract against potential loss arising from the default of a counterparty or a security – AIG was able to in effect own that niche. Its status as an insurer meant it was subject to different regulatory oversight than banks. In addition, as a result of evolving regulations, from 2000, CDSs had in effect fallen into a regulatory gap as they were not classed as either securities or insurance contracts. This allowed AIG to underwrite increasing amounts of CDSs without any regulator taking a particularly keen interest and without any related reporting and capital requirements.

So, by the end of 2007, AIG had $1 trillion in assets, shareholders' funds of ~$96 billion, market capitalization of $150 billion and when the financial crisis hit in 2008, it had written CDSs on over $500 billion of assets. Part of this exposure to CDSs concerned collateralized debt obligations (CDOs) which included residential mortgage-backed securities (RMBS) and in some of these RMBSs there were also subprime mortgages. Consequently, when first Bear Stearns and then Lehman Brothers collapsed due to the problems of the subprime mortgage market, AIG found itself with an exposure of ~$78 billion of CDSs poisoned by toxic subprime mortgage securities. In parallel, it saw its liquidity drain away as counterparties who had borrowed securities from it and had posted cash as collateral, started returning the securities and requesting their cash back.

The liquidity situation became critical very quickly since AIG had actually used some of the cash to invest in precisely the type of mortgage-backed securities that were being affected by the market turmoil. So, the U.S. government stepped in with a two-year credit line of $85 billion to allow AIG to liquidate some of its $1 trillion in assets and repay creditors whilst at the same time honouring its obligations on CDSs it had written to some of the biggest banks and investment banks around the world. At the time it was estimated that if AIG failed to live up to its CDS obligations, there would have a been a ~$180 billion black hole affecting the biggest banks and investments banks which could draw more financial institutions into bankruptcy. In the end, the package of assistance from the authorities expanded to the tune of $182 billion and AIG used about $126 billion.

Were there any observable signals that could have foretold the troubles that lay ahead? In the financial markets it was common knowledge that AIG was a very big underwriter of CDSs. So, at least some financial players were aware that AIG could find itself in trouble if it ever had to pay under these CDSs, particularly with respect to the RMBSs with subprime mortgages. It was also commonly felt that AIG, taking its lead from its long tenured CEO, Maurice "Hank" Greenberg, was generally quite an aggressive player in all its activities. Greenberg, had led AIG for over 40 years and had gradually become its largest single shareholder, perhaps in itself a red flag for some, yet a positive in many investors' score card for aligning his interests with those of their own as shareholders.

But the near collapse in 2008 was not the first time AIG had flirted with controversy and had faced issues with regulators. In 2003, 2004 and 2005, the SEC had levelled charges of fraud against AIG. In each case, AIG was accused of engaging in accounting and other practices that concealed losses or flattered earnings and therefore issuing misleading financial statements. In 2003, the matter was settled through a civil penalty of $10 million. The 2004 charge was settled with AIG paying disgorgements and penalty of $126 million. In early 2006, AIG settled the 2005 SEC charges by agreeing to pay $800 million, consisting of $700 million disgorgements and a $100 million fine. Some, understandably, would claim that the nature and frequency of SEC charges should have served as red flags that AIG was prepared to sail very close to the regulatory winds and was not averse to cutting some corners if there was the possibility of getting away with it or only facing a fine it could afford to pay. Others would point to the Chairman and CEO, his long tenure and the culture he promoted as both red flags and factors which contributed to the excessive risk taking in the underregulated niche of CDS that brought AIG to its knees.

2.3.2.2. Red flags for banks

As is the case for industrial companies, spotting red flags in banks which could foretell future problems also requires attention to practically all aspects of a company's operations, governance arrangements, culture, and M&A activity, among other things. The list below is also illustrative and not an exhaustive checklist. As previously, it is intended to highlight the frame of mind one has to adopt and the nature of signals one has to become sensitive to, in order to recognize red flags in a timely fashion.

- ➢ Balance sheet imbalances – too many deposits relative to loans creating incentives to take on more and more risk; too few deposits relative to loans creating reliance on unstable sources of funding
- ➢ Trading culture and importance of proprietary trading to results – this can create a temptation to make up for shortfalls elsewhere and increases the volatility of earnings
- ➢ Aggressive expansion of loan portfolio – this can be particularly telling if counter to economic cycle
- ➢ Aggressive international expansion – What is the source of competitive advantage in foreign markets?
- ➢ Related party lending – big loans to shareholders, directors and their families or associates, which usually have to be reported in the bank's financial statements
- ➢ Boards with non-executives with no real experience of banking
- ➢ Frequent capital raising and conversion of deposits to risk securities, especially if involving offers for better interest at no extra risk
- ➢ Culture of cutting corners and absence of controls – loose documentation, loose enforcement of standards, variable standards
- ➢ Large bonuses to executives as incentives can encourage excessive short-term risk taking
- ➢ Growth via aggressive and contested acquisitions, particularly if at historically high valuations
- ➢ Public sparring with regulators or worse investigations and/or fines by regulators relating to accounting matters
- ➢ Long tenured, empire building CEOs promoting culture of opaqueness or anything goes in the pursuit of profit

Notwithstanding looking out for red flags, as regulators also recognize, banking sector crises are to be expected from time to time, as banks are always ahead of the regulators and regulations usually deal with the causes of the last crisis rather than the next one. Thus, beyond looking out for red flags, companies need to protect themselves from banking sector problems including through:

- ✓ Diversification of banking relationships by establishing such relationships at the domestic and international level
- ✓ Diversification of financing and funding instruments by using banking products as well as capital markets

✓ Limiting reliance on and exposure to banks
✓ Awareness of banking sector developments/ trends and red flags and periodic assessment of exposure levels

2.3.3. Lessons for Boards from failures during transitions

In a six-year research study which culminated in a bestselling book published in 2003, *Why Smart Executives Fail*, Sydney Finkelstein, a chaired professor for Strategy at Amos Tuck Business School, collected and analysed the failures of a large number of companies and came to a very interesting conclusion. Though the companies analysed were in different industries and even countries, their failures occurred in the context of transitions they were undergoing and which presented challenges that when not met, led to failure. These transitions fitted into four different types:

a. Creating successful new ventures

The pursuit of new businesses is usually resource intensive but when successful, it can reinvigorate a company and can contribute to its longevity. But, if it becomes an obsessive chimera which is not grounded in reality, it consumes resources a company can ill afford and leads to failure. There is no substitute for careful analysis and due diligence before embarking on such a challenging transition of building a new business as well as during the implementation phase. Surveying market conditions before launch of a new venture is a necessary condition but it is not sufficient for success. Market conditions can change before the new business reaches maturity and that can lead to catastrophic failure. Iridium, a company that raised and deployed billions of dollars in the late 1990s failed before the new millennium when its quest to deliver mobile telephony connectivity via satellites by charging customers $3,000 for a handset and $3–8 per minute for calls, became irrelevant to consumers as the cellular mobile phone connectivity delivered a better quality of service than its satellite alternative at a lower cost. Simply put, the founder, management and Board of Iridium had not taken into account that the competing technologies were likely to improve and anyway requesting users of Iridium services to seek line of sight with their satellites in order to make or receive a call was never going to represent value for money for at least 50,000 subscribers they needed to ensure sufficient cashflow to meet debt covenants. The company only managed to get 20,000 customers and filed for Chapter 11 bankruptcy protection in August 1999.

b. Managing Mergers & Acquisitions (M&A)

M&As are a recognized and often used path to growth. And growth is considered one of the contributors to longevity. Companies that become adept at mergers and acquisitions can come from humble beginnings to dominate entire industries. My own career started with Chemical Bank in New York in 1987 when it was one of many New York banks with ambition and a balance sheet. They merged with Manufacturers Hanover Trust in 1992 and kept the Chemical brand. Then, in 1996 when Chemical was the third largest bank in the US, it merged with Chase Manhattan Bank and dropped the Chemical Bank name as Chase Manhattan was considered the more recognized brand, particularly internationally. The combined entity was the largest bank in the US. Finally, in 2000, Chase Manhattan merged with JP Morgan to create JP Morgan Chase, the largest financial institution in the US, which has remained a dominant force in US and global banking since. But M&As are transitions fraught with integration challenges. Many small details need to be addressed well otherwise they can have large negative consequences. And if the acquisition is executed at a valuation that is too rich and at a time that the market may be about to turn, it can spell disaster for the acquiring firm's shareholders who then legitimately ask questions of the management and the Board. Royal Bank of Scotland's pursuit and acquisition of ABN AMRO certainly fits in that category. Time Warner's 2000 $350 billion merger with internet service provider AOL, valuing AOL at $182 billion and handing 55% of the combined entity to AOL's shareholders despite Time Warner being the more established company with greater revenues and assets is another where the acquired company's shareholders were handed riches from the jaws of oblivion whilst the acquiring company's shareholders ceded value in pursuit of a CEO's empire building on a massive scale. The $350 billion merger soured quickly as the internet bubble burst and eventually AOL was demerged in 2009 and then acquired by Verizon Communications for $4.4 billion in 2015. Time Warner was itself taken over in 2016 by AT&T for $85 billion, which fought the Department of Justice for years in order to finally consummate the deal in 2018. In 2021, ATT announced the merger of WarnerMedia with the Discovery media company to form a new, separate entity potentially worth as much as $150 billion including debt, in which the shareholders of ATT will retain 71% and also benefit from $43 billion of cash and retention of debt by the new entity.

c. Dealing with innovation and change

We have already encountered examples of companies, such as Nokia and Research In Motion, who were once lauded for their innovation but failed to keep innovating in order to cater to the changing needs and preferences of their customers. We can add the even earlier leader in the mobile phone pack who were the leader in analogue devices and networks in the world in the mid-1990s and had experienced impressive average annual growth of 27% in revenues and 58% in net income between 1992 and 1995. They had the technical capability to migrate to digital hand sets and networks and at least engage with their emerging competition, but chose not to, even as they understood the economics of the digital technology were far more favourable for networks since they could pack ten times more subscribers on the same physical infrastructure than analogue counterparts. They were quickly overtaken by Nokia which came to dominate the mobile phone market for years, until the next technological innovation wave of the smartphones. As a former CEO of Motorola acknowledged in 2001, "Some of the leadership in the business at that time was focused too much on the short-term profits and they weren't spending enough for the future." The decentralized management structure of Motorola and operating division-based incentives had also played its part in breeding a tribe mentality instead of collaboration for the common good amongst its operating divisions. In the end, the transition to digital cell phones was delayed, at least in part, because of the short-term negative effects on divisional profit and losses arising from the investment needed.

d. Developing winning strategies in the face of new competitive pressures

Strategy is what a company does or does not do in order to fulfil its vision in a competitive marketplace. A solid strategy addresses who you are selling to, what you are selling to them and how you are selling. A sustainable strategy is based on real competence that customers value enough to pay for and competitors cannot copy or improve on. Forgetting the above simple truths about strategy can lead to companies pursuing and implementing strategies which can disconnect them from their markets and customers with catastrophic results.

The An Wang story of rags to riches and then bankruptcy has echoes of Research In Motion, Digital Equipment Corporation and Nokia. It is a story of an inability to develop a new winning strategy for a changing competitive landscape. Wang was the founder of Wang Labs who first developed magnetic tape as a storage medium for computer processing. He followed that up with a desktop calculator and then developed dedicated word processing machines that came to dominate the industry. At its peak it generated $210 million net income in 1984 on $2.1 billion of sales. But, its specialization on word processor computers became its millstone in the late 1980s when personal computers became available with operating systems that turned the PCs into general purpose personal computers. Profits turned to losses from 1986 onwards after a desperate last-ditch effort to stem its losses by partnering in 1991 with IBM to sell IBM machines along with Wang customized software to support them, it filed for bankruptcy in 1992. It had lost a cumulative $1.665 billion from 1989 to its eventual collapse. The company and its founder had proven incapable of dealing with the emerging threat of the general-purpose personal computer.

It is very clear from the preceding examples that a Board really does need to earn its keep when faced with such transition challenges. Directors' antennae inside and outside the company need to be on full alert. CEOs and management teams should not be given any free passes by their Boards in explaining themselves and their plans for transitions and the associated challenges. The allocation of resources to meet such challenges and at the same time preserve or enhance shareholder value is firmly within the remit of a Board. A Board would be abdicating its responsibility in this respect if it does not scrutinize plans relating to transitions to satisfy itself that:

➤ assumptions underpinning new ventures are grounded in reality, both at the outset and by the time the plans are implemented
➤ a merger or an acquisition generates rather than detracts value for shareholders
➤ innovation and change is embraced in order to ensure the company's product and services positioning remains aligned to evolving customers' needs and preferences
➤ strategy remains aligned with market opportunity which may be changing as a result of new competitive pressures

A Board is well advised to be cautious to the point of being paranoid about transitions and heed the advice of legendary Intel Corporation CEO, Andy Grove, who published a book in 1988 titled *Only the Paranoid Survive*.

2.3.4. Red flags from leaders' habits and lessons for Boards

In the same book that demonstrated that certain transitions need to attract special attention from management and the Board of a company, Sydney Finkelstein also identified seven habits that characterised leaders who presided over major business failures. These were:

1. "They see themselves and their companies dominating their environments, not simply responding to developments in those environments"
2. "They identify so completely with the company that there is no clear boundary between their personal interests and the corporate interests"
3. "They seem to have all the answers, often dazzling people with the speed and decisiveness with which they can deal with challenging issues"
4. "They make sure that everyone is 100% behind them, ruthlessly eliminate anyone who might undermine their efforts"
5. "They are consummate company spokespersons, often devoting the largest portion of their efforts to managing and developing the company image"
6. "They treat intimidatingly difficult obstacles as temporary impediments to be removed or overcome"
7. "They never hesitate to return to strategies and tactics that made them and their companies successful in the first place"

It is arguable that at least some of these traits are useful to aspiring leaders on their way to the top, for example seeking to dominate a market through innovation can be a very positive habit. Entrepreneurs who see their businesses as extensions of themselves and live by the motto failure is not an option, can be inspiring leaders and build very successful businesses. Leaders who ensure their teams are fully behind them may credit such unity and commitment to the cause for speedier responses to challenges and faster implementation of plans. Indeed, each of these habits can be seen in a positive as well as a negative light, not only for leaders on their way to the top but also when they are already at the top. But the way these habits harden over time, particularly as a result of early success can lead to them becoming corrosive influences on the way companies are actually ran by leaders exhibiting all or different combinations of these habits. The bottom line is that if they are left unchecked by a pliant Board or worse reinforced by a sycophantic Board, they can breed arrogance and complacency not only at the top but throughout the organization.

For example, if on the back of their past success CEOs come to believe they are truly masters of their market and know better than anyone plus demand complete loyalty and brook no argument or question of their tried and tested methods, yet the company they lead is facing competitors who are out-innovating the company, who, if not the Board, will provide the wake-up call before it's too late? We have already encountered a version of this narrative in how Research In Motion, lauded for bringing the BlackBerry smartphone to market, was too slow to react to the iPhone and the touch screen that sealed its permanent decline from its market position.

If the executive management of a company comes to believe they are synonymous with a product or a service and cannot bring themselves to recognize a new product or service that could render them irrelevant to their customers' needs, who, if not the Board, will challenge the management on their arrogant and complacent assumptions and behaviour? This is a narrative that could fit a number of bygone companies like makers of minicomputers such as Digital Equipment Corporation who dominated that market segment but did not migrate into personal computers and instead kept trying to find a new niche for minicomputers, or makers of photographic film such as Kodak, who had every opportunity but chose not to adopt to the tsunami of digital photography.

A Board which recognizes signs of the habits already listed in the company's leader or management, needs to become more vigilant in their scrutiny of their plans, their analyses and their actions. Board members, individually and collectively, need to use their own experience and observations from outside the company and become more willing to ask tougher questions and challenge assumptions more robustly. Fundamentally, they must recognize that part of the job is to recognize reality and make sure the CEO and the management do the same. They have a duty to speak truth to power and serve the company by being a true check on the CEO and executive management team. When necessary, they must be willing to point the nudity of the emperor rather than behave as part of their entourage. They must be prepared to seek the bad news, to listen to negative developments and elicit constructive responses. And if the CEO is not willing to be checked or is incapable of being checked, then the Board's fiduciary duty should include triggering the ultimate sanction of replacement. Sadly, as history shows, too many Boards of companies that have failed under CEOs who exhibited these habits were unable to take such corrective action.

2.4. Chapter closing thoughts

Practitioners of good Corporate Governance are better equipped to anticipate problems and manage risk that may arise from failures of Corporate Governance in clients, suppliers, service providers and banks. In short it pays to practice good Corporate Governance. When it comes to looking out for red flags, the old adage that a fish spoils at the head first is worth keeping in mind. Corporate Governance deficiencies and failures are all too often associated with leaders who may have paid lip service to Corporate Governance in having Boards and committees but were never constrained by such governance arrangements and rather behaved as if they felt the rules were not meant to apply to them as to everyone else.

Chapter 3:
Family Business and Corporate Governance

3.1. Brief definition of Family Business and types of family businesses

There is o single type of family business and it is a truism that every family business is unique in its own unique way. But there are at least two ways to characterize a business that is controlled by a family that can allow some useful groupings of family businesses to be identified. Firstly, there is the dimension of ownership and the generation of the family that controls the business. And secondly, there is the relative priority that the family interests and needs take in relation to the business's interests and needs. Where a family business lies in the spectrum on these two dimensions can have profound implications on the nature of Corporate Governance that is appropriate for the particular family business and how Corporate Governance is practiced, if at all.

3.1.1. Types of family business based on ownership

A family business is commonly understood to be a business controlled by a family. When such a business is organized as a company, the voting majority is in the hands of the controlling family, including the founders who intend to pass the business on to their descendants. However, under this simple and broad, umbrella-like definition, one can identify different types of family business which are linked to their ownership structure and which exhibit their own characteristics. As illustrated in the diagram below, family-controlled businesses can be listed on stock exchanges or privately-held. If privately-held, it is possible that the family owns the business 100% or controls it without necessarily owning 100% of the shares.

Beyond the private vs. public ownership dimension, another key characteristic of a family business is the generation of the company that controls the company. Along this dimension, firstly there are family businesses which are controlled by their founder. Secondly, there are family businesses which are controlled and managed by the children of the founder in a "sibling partnership" arrangement. Thirdly, there are family businesses whose longevity means their ownership is spread amongst multiple family members that extend to a third generation, i.e. cousins who are grandchildren of the original founder. And so on, to the nth generation of descendants of the founders.

Figure 3.1.1.a. Types of family-controlled businesses

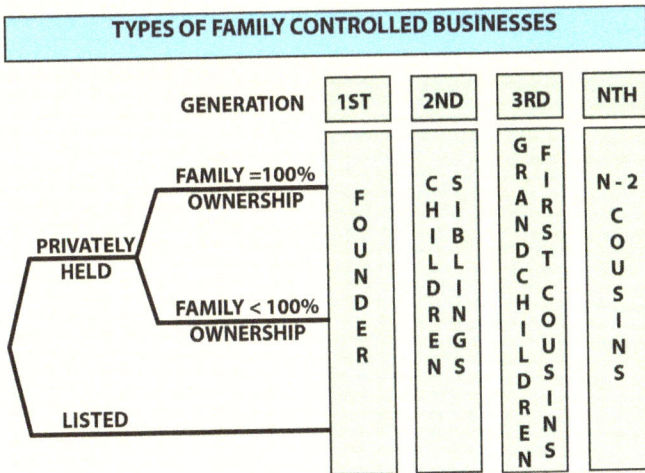

3.1.2. Types of family business based on priorities

Running any business requires policies on a number of critical dimensions including:

- ✓ Employment policy – who gets employed by the business?
- ✓ Compensation policy – how is compensation determined for each employee?
- ✓ Capital resources allocation policy – how are the resources of the business deployed?
- ✓ Training – how is training viewed and implemented?
- ✓ Leadership – how is the leadership of the business determined?

In formulating policies along these critical dimensions, families who control businesses have a crucial choice to make in terms of what they prioritize. Do they prioritize the needs of the family or the needs of the business?

In family businesses where the family needs come first, when it comes to employment policy, a family member would have an automatic right to be employed by the family business because he or she is a family member irrespective of the needs of the business at the particular point in time. In such family businesses, the business accommodates the needs of the family. By contrast, a family business where the needs of the business take priority, a family member would not have such an automatic right of employment in the family business. Instead, their employment would be conditioned by the needs of the business and the matching of their skills and experiences to the requirements of the particular job opening. The business would not be accommodating the needs of the family but taking care of its own needs for its own financial well-being.

When it comes to compensation policy, in a "Family First" family business, the compensation for all family members may be set at the same level irrespective of relative responsibilities and contributions. Such a policy can of course be detrimental in terms of motivation and incentivization of family and non-family employees alike. It may be set also in accordance to the needs of the family employees in order to fund a desired lifestyle. Such a policy could overstretch the finances of the family business if the compensation to family members proves beyond the sustainable means of the family business. In a "Business First" family business, there would be various safeguards when designing the compensation policy of the business in order to ensure it has the desired impact on motivation and incentives and long-term sustainability.

In the area of capital resources allocation, a crucial distinction between the Family First family businesses and Business First family businesses is who is meant to benefit from the deployment of such resources. In Family First family businesses, often capital resources are used for the needs of the family, which under certain circumstances (e.g. family businesses with owners and creditors who are non-family members) can stray into being illegal and can prove catastrophic if abused (e.g. the Adelphia case – please see section 3.2.2.1). By contrast, in Business First family businesses, the use of capital resources is focused on advancing the interests of the business.

In terms of training, a Family First orientation may mean absence of any training as the family members are expected to take on their roles like ducks to water – "It runs in the DNA" being a frequent belief underpinning such disregard for formal training. A Business First orientation will usually mean recognition of the vital role training can play for both family and non-family senior executives, even Board members.

Finally, in Family First family businesses, leadership is reserved for family members, often in line with seniority and tenure instead of commitment and ability to actually provide effective leadership. By contrast, in Business First family businesses, a great deal of thought goes into succession planning and selection of leadership, with the accident of birth taking a much lower rating in the calculations.

As one can see from the summary table below, along each of these critical dimensions, one can see clear differences in how Family First family businesses and Business First family businesses strike the balance between family and business interests and priorities.

Figure 3.1.2.a. Policies in family businesses – Family First Vs Business First

Differences in policies of Family First Family Businessess and Business First Family Businesses		
ISSUE	**FAMILY FIRST COMPANIES**	**BUSINESS FIRST COMPANIES**
Employment Policy	Open door policy for all family members The family busines becomes safety net for those who cannot succeed outside the business Family members do not get fired	Only qualified family members enter the company Conditions of family employment are clearly set and include education and outside the family business work experience requirements
Compensation	Equal pay for all family members - everyone paid the same regardless of their experience and contribution to the business Competent family members are expected to care (via compensation, benefits etc.) for their less competent siblings or cousins	Compensation is based on performance and responsibility Compensation is based on market and industry measures, not on family needs Accountabilities and reporting relationship are clearly communicated and understood High performances are highly paid Family members can be fired for poor performance
Leadership	Leadership is based on seniority rather than demonstrated competence or successess Longevity in the family business may be more valued than working and succeeding outside the family business	Positions of leadership filled on merit, irrespective of family connection The family mantra is to have "the best and the brightest" running the business, irrespective of family links Non-family senior executives may be recruited from within the industry or grown internally
Business Resources Allocation	Business resources are used for family members' personal needs (e.g. housing, cars, personal purchases, investments etc.)	Business resources are used strategically There is clear separation of business and family assets. Budgeting and planning are important. Profits are used for growth initiatives or paid out as dividends
Training	No formal training programs. Family members are expected to intuitively learn business practices	Need for formal and timely training is recognised. Trainings are scheduled and delivered to teach family members business practices

3.2. Overview of family business

3.2.1. Role of family business in economy

Family businesses are the oldest and most dominant form of business organizations. In the USA, according to the U.S. Bureau of the Census, about 90% of American businesses are family-owned or controlled. Ranging in size from two-person partnerships to Fortune 500 firms, these businesses account for half of the nation's employment and half of the United States' GDP. In the UK, the Institute for Family Business estimates that family firms contributed about one-third of UK GDP and paid a quarter of the tax receipts. In Germany, it is estimated that the top 500 German family businesses contribute over 40% of the country's GDP. In China, family businesses share of GDP is estimated at over 50%. In Spain, family businesses represent around two-thirds of GDP and in Latin America around 60% of GDP. Globally, in 2019, the largest 750 family-controlled businesses, generated over $10 trillion in revenues compared with $87.5 trillion of global GDP.

Despite their importance as engines of individual countries and the global economy, family businesses tend to have a short lifespan. In fact, the majority of family businesses do not survive to the third generation of family ownership. Whilst statistics vary from country to country, generally less than a third of businesses transition from the founder to the second generation and only about an eighth of businesses make it from the founder to the third generation of the family. Despite the low survival rate, studies in a number of countries (including the US, UK, Germany, Switzerland, Italy and Spain) have shown that family businesses outperform their non-family counterparts in terms of sales, profits and other growth measures. Moreover, family businesses which do survive long term often become national institutions, often almost synonymous with the founder's country. For example, consider Ford Motors (US), AP Moller-Maersk (Denmark), Henkel (Germany), Siemens (Germany), Carrefour (France), LVMH (France), Samsung (Korea), Hyundai (Korea), Toyota (Japan) and Kikkoman (Japan).

What is the reason that despite their obvious dynamism, most family businesses do not make it to the third generation? In our view the low survival rates of family businesses is a reflection of the unique governance challenges they face, in respect of Corporate Governance and Family Governance. Later chapters on the book expand on how good Corporate Governance and Family Governance enhance the prospects of a family business becoming multigenerational.

3.2.2. Strengths and weaknesses of the family business

3.2.2.1. Strengths of the family business

A family business can benefit from strong commitment from its owning family which remains dedicated to the business as it grows and gets passed onto the next generation. Many family members come to identify with their particular company and are willing to work harder and reinvest more of their profits into growing the business over the long term. This strong commitment from their owners, is one of the strengths of family businesses.

Another strength is the continuity of the knowledge, experience and skills that gets passed to the next generations of the owning family. As older generations remain engaged and provide valuable memories, experiences and contacts, and as many family members get immersed in their family's business from a young age, there is often a protracted transition bridge which non-family companies cannot recreate very easily.

Finally, families controlling businesses are usually sensitive and protective of their reputation and name. They strive to maintain and increase the quality of their products and services, and to maintain a good relationship with their partners (for example customers, employees, suppliers and community) since this is a way to safeguard not only the fortunes of the business but also their own name which they may be sharing with the family company.

3.2.2.2. Weaknesses of the family business

As already mentioned, many family businesses fail to be sustainable in the long term and about two-thirds of family businesses either collapse or are sold by their founders during their lifetime. The reasons contributing to family businesses failing include some of the same reasons as for non-family businesses, like poor management, lack of growth capital and financing, inadequate cost controls, industry trends and other macro conditions. But in addition, family businesses that do not make it to the third generation also show some specific weaknesses that are especially relevant to their nature.

Firstly, *complexity*. For a start, family businesses are usually more complex in terms of governance than their counterparts due to the addition of the family into the equation.

Secondly, *informality*. As most families run their businesses themselves (at least during the first and second generations) there is usually little interest in setting clearly articulated business practices and procedures; as a family and its business grow larger, this informality can lead to many inefficiencies and internal conflicts that can threaten the continuity of the business.

Thirdly – *lack of discipline*. Many family businesses do not pay sufficient attention to key strategic areas such as CEO and senior management succession planning, attracting and retaining skilled outside managers, family employment, etc.

3.3. Interactions between a family and the business controlled by the family

3.3.1. Multiplicity of roles of family members and impact on governance challenges

A family can interact in multiple ways with a business it controls. Some of the roles that an owner (i.e. a shareholder) in a family business can have include:

- ✓ Owner only with no active involvement in either management or governance of the company and no role in the affairs of the family – this is sometimes a role taken by a son, daughter, grandson or grand-daughter of a founder who have been given shares in the family business, or a founder who has retired and withdrawn from all affairs of the company and the family
- ✓ Owner and also manager with active involvement in the management

but not in the governance of the company or the affairs of the family – this is often the role adopted by a son or daughter, grandson or granddaughter of a founder who have been given shares in the family business and have assumed the duties of a senior manager, but are not yet a director of the company or a member of the family's governance arrangements

✓ Owner and also manager with active involvement in the company and also a family member with an active role in the affairs of the family – this can be a founder who has not yet adopted a formal Board for the Corporate Governance arrangement of the company, i.e. there are no directors as such in the company, or a family member who is active in senior management and the affairs of the family but not yet a director in the company's Board

✓ Owner and also director but not actively involved in management – this can be the role adopted by a founder after they have passed on the managerial responsibility to another family member

✓ Owner and also a director and actively involved in the family's affairs but not involved in a management capacity in the company – this may be the role of family members who have brought into the business non-family members to act as managers, or simply family members who are not in the business full time and can act as directors whilst other family members who are in the business full time take on the managerial responsibilities

✓ Owner and also active in the family's affairs, along with being a director and a manager of the family-controlled company – this can be the role assumed by the founder or a member of the next generations who is actively involved in the business.

Of course, this multiplicity of potential ways that family members can interact with the family's business, is a reflection of the fact that as family businesses progress into future generations, there will always be family members who will not wish to be involved full time with the family business but will retain their ownership interest and possibly also a role in the governance of the family business or the family's own affairs.

The corollary of the multiple roles and responsibilities that family members can have which can be associated also with different incentives and controls, both for active and nonactive family members as well as for family and non-family counterparts, is that they increase and complicate the governance challenge for family businesses. In fact, this multiplicity of roles and interactions make it imperative that a family finds a way to regulate these interactions in ways that are strengthening rather than weakening the family business.

How a family organizes its family members' interactions with the family business can indeed influence the prospects of both the family and the business it controls. Owning families who put the needs of the business first, can be described as operating a business-oriented family business. On the other hand, owning families who organize the business to suit the needs of the family, can be described as operating a family-oriented family business.

3.3.2. Distinction between family and business assets

One key interaction between a family and the business it controls, concerns the treatment of the business assets by the family. Even in cases where a family business is 100% owned and controlled by the family, the family must never forget that the assets of a company do not belong to the family. Once a company has been formed and assets and liabilities created on its balance sheet, the owners of the business cannot treat the assets as their own since the company's creditors actually have a priority claim on the company's assets ahead of its shareholders. And in the absence of commercial creditors, the owners of the business still rank behind the tax authorities. It is a shortcut to disaster for a family to forget this rule.

3.3.2.1. The Adelphia fraud case – the rise and fall of the Rigas family –

John Rigas and his brother Gus had started a small Pennsylvania town cable TV business with $300 in 1952 and over a 50-year period, John had turned this into the NASDAQ listed cable titan Adelphia Communications with over 2 million cable TV subscribers. Apart from cable TV, Adelphia was also an early provider of high-speed internet as well as phone services and mobile messaging for businesses. The company was one of the top 10 cable TV operators in the US and was admired for its high operating margins, often attributed to the fact its systems were all clustered on the East Coast. The company had kept its headquarters at the small town of Coudersport, Pennsylvania, where it had all started. John Rigas was running the company along with his four well educated sons who were all Board members and the family was considered a great benefactor of the town of Coudersport and its people, with their charitable giving and sponsorship of events for the town. The Rigases were billionaires and also owners of the Buffalo Sabres NHL ice-hockey team.

From the beginning of his business journey, John Rigas had not been averse to borrowing massive amounts of money to fund the expansion of his business. Even as a publicly listed company, Adelphia stood out amongst its peers for its aggressive use of leverage. In 1996, Adelphia's debt was 11 times its market capitalization. By contrast, Comcast's ratio was 1.28 and Cox Communications was 0.45. At the time, analysts felt that this great overhang of debt was causing the stock of Adelphia to trade at a great discount to net asset value. John Rigas and his family did not seem to care about the stock price of the business they still controlled via class B voting shares they owned. The company did not pay a dividend and John Rigas and his sons were paid modest amounts from the company, yet the Rigas family had a luxurious lifestyle.

Then in May 2002, it all came crashing down and suddenly the world had a different view of what the Rigas family had been up to. The unravelling began in March 2002, when the company's CFO, one of Rigas's sons, had to acknowledge the company had $2.3 billion of off-balance sheet loans which had funded Rigas family's purchases of Adelphia stock and convertible bonds. As the convertible bonds had halved in value, the company was facing a very significant deficit since the borrowings were taken by the Rigas family with the company as the backstop source of repayment if the Rigases failed to meet their loan obligations. Quickly after that the independent directors began to realize that funds they thought were intended for cable system acquisitions had instead been used by the family for the family's own investments in the company's stock. As the bankruptcy became inevitable, the banks conditioned further lending to the company on the resignation and relinquishing of control by the Rigas family, in order to enter Chapter 11 with a chance to exit it in orderly fashion. In May 2002, John Rigas and his sons did resign and relinquish control and the SEC initiated an investigation. In 2007, John Rigas and his CFO son Tim Rigas were sentenced to 15- and 20-year prison sentences for their role in the looting and debt hiding that had taken place. It turned out the charity giving by the family was in fact paid for by the company. Personal luxury purchases to the tune of $100 million were also funded by the company without the independent directors approving any of them. The SEC described the scandal as "one of the most extensive financial frauds ever to take place at a public company."

At his trial John Rigas he told the judge "In my heart and in my conscience, I'll go to my grave really and truly believing that I did nothing but try to improve the conditions of my employees. If I did anything wrong, I apologize." His defence counsel pointed to his deep involvement in philanthropy. The judge's view was that "To be a great philanthropist with other people's money really is not very persuasive".

Where did it all go wrong? The aggressive use of leverage was always going to put the company in a precarious financial position. That could be considered a failure in Corporate Governance. But there were other elements that blurred the distinction between the family and the company. A Rigas family member was both the CFO of the listed company and Chairman of the Board Audit Committee which normally keeps the CFO of a company accountable. This was another failure in Corporate Governance. But the key element that caused the collapse was that the family had failed to remember that company assets were not family assets. There were other shareholders and creditors who had an economic interest in these assets and they were not to be handled by the family for its own benefit.

3.4. Corporate Governance in family-controlled businesses

Corporate Governance in family-controlled businesses concerns the interaction of the company with its shareholders and the oversight of management exercised by an oversight body on behalf of the shareholders in the same way that we have encountered already in Chapter 1. Under the shareholder level, it also concerns Risk Management and Internal Audit in the same way we have also encountered in Chapter 1.

Depending on the legal form the family-controlled business takes, the nature of the oversight body we encounter in a family-controlled business is heavily influenced by requirements set down by law and regulations for that particular legal form. In many jurisdictions, laws and regulations prescribe the minimum size of an oversight body for a particular legal form as well as their minimum duties particularly vis-à-vis third parties and stakeholders (for example responsibility for tax returns, environmental compliance, health and safety compliance and the like). At the same time, the preferences of the controlling family also heavily influence the attributes of the particular oversight body since it is the family that decides the actual size and determines the composition of the oversight body. In family-controlled businesses with good Corporate Governance, a third driver are the prevailing perceptions of what constitute good Corporate Governance standards.

Figure 3.4.a. Drivers of Corporate Governance in family-controlled businesses

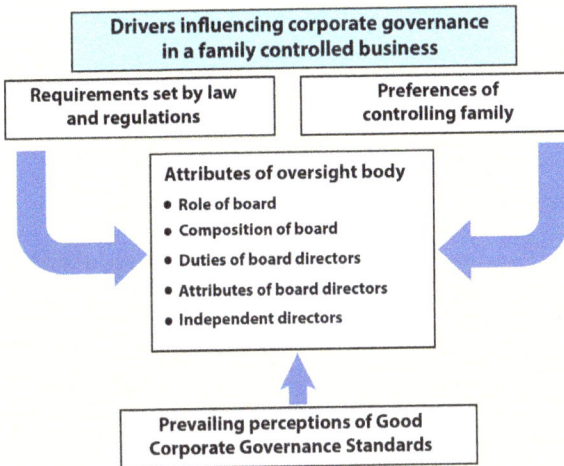

3.4.1. Types of oversight bodies in family-controlled businesses

Even if the duties and responsibilities of an oversight body are set down in law and by regulations, the composition of such a body can greatly influence their value-add in practice. Thus, one can distinguish at least three different types of oversight bodies in different family-controlled businesses or even in the same business at different points in their evolution.

3.4.1.1. Paper or Rubberstamp Board of Directors

When Boards are created merely in order to comply with legal requirements but with little value added, they are known as "paper Boards" or "rubberstamp Boards". Such paper or rubberstamp Boards are still the bodies that approve financials, dividends, tax returns and other items requiring Board approval by law, but as the name implies do little else. They do not get involved in strategy formulation, capital allocation or senior management hiring and firing and succession planning. Paper or rubberstamp Boards typically meet relatively infrequently (once or twice a year depending on local regulation) and meetings are typically very short in duration. They are usually composed exclusively of family members of the controlling family, though occasionally they may include a few trusted senior managers. It is very common for the same individuals to be owners, managers and directors.

Boards of this nature provide no real separation between Board, management and owning family. Thus as a governance structure, these Boards, add little value to the family business since the individual elements (Board, management, ownership) overlap and cannot play separate and constructive role within a balanced governance arrangement. Overall, such Boards do not have the capacity to act as a counterweight to a founder or a family's wishes and whims, and consequently their value-add does not extend much beyond ensuring compliance with laws and regulations requiring the existence of an oversight body.

Despite their lack of true value added, Boards of this type can nevertheless be relevant and even appropriate in some circumstances. A family corner shop may not need much more than exactly such a Board. Similarly, in the very early days of a new business venture, an entrepreneur may not even be able to recruit anyone other than family to serve on a Board.

3.4.1.2. Advisory Boards

Whilst families may use paper or rubberstamp Boards to ensure compliance, they may recognize the need for some value-add from an oversight body but still not be comfortable with sharing sensitive information and decision-making power with outsiders at Board level. In such circumstances, family-controlled business may use in parallel to the paper or rubberstamp Board of a family company, an Advisory Board which does include some independent, non-family members. Such Advisory Boards are often considered a compromise or transition solution between a family dominated oversight body and an oversight body with true decision-making powers which includes non-family members. As the name implies, Advisory Boards, particularly if composed of experienced and respected individuals, including from outside the family, are used as sounding Boards and are intended to compensate for the potential shortcomings of the actual Boards of Directors, which remain only composed of family members.

Advisory Boards are usually composed of three to seven members and bring relevant expertise in the industry or market segment of the family business or in functional areas such as finance, marketing and international markets. They tend to meet three to four times a year with the Chairman or CEO of the family business plus a few senior managers from the family business.

In order to safeguard objectivity Advisory Boards should not include

- Suppliers or vendors to the company
- Friends of the owners with no relevant expertise to offer
- Existing providers of services to the company (e.g. bankers, lawyers, external auditors, consultants) since their advice is already provided in other forms and their independence may be questionable
- Individuals who have a conflict of interest in being advisors to the company
- Individuals who are already overcommitted and would not be able to devote sufficient time

Advisory Boards can serve a useful function and add value but they are not without their own drawbacks. As highlighted in the table below, Advisory Boards can provide at least some of the benefits of an oversight body with some degree of independence and at less cost than a more formal Board of Directors. But, as they lack true legal standing, they are limited to being consultative without true decision-making powers, which to a degree dilutes their benefits. Still, families and founders who treat Advisory Boards with respect and take their advice seriously are in a better position than those who rely entirely on paper or rubberstamp Boards or set up Advisory Boards simply to tick a box.

Figure 3.4.1.2.a. Advantages and Disadvantages of Advisory Boards

Advantages and Disadvantages of Advisory Boards	
Advantages	**Disadvantages**
+ Its members have no legal responsibility and this reduces the company's cost (e.g. no insurance necessary) and makes it easier to recruit members (since membership is not as risky as being part of the company's Board of Directors) + Can provide the company with additional skills, technical expertise and knowledge that are not available at the current management and board levels + Its advice is usually unbiassed + Its members may offer new contacts that can lead to additional sales or sources of capital	– The Advisory Board functions like a group of experts whose advice is not systematically followed by the company; As a consequence, the Advisory Board may not be taken as seriously as a real Board of Directors – The Advisory Board has no authority to request information from the management, so its recommendation can only be based on what management is willing to share with its members – Advisory Board members have little or no influence on the strategy and the oversight of the management – The lack of legal responsibility makes it difficult to hold members of the Advisory Board accountable for their advice – Some Advisory Board members might not take their roles seriously and put in the necessary preparation and contribution as they would as real Board members

3.4.1.3. Boards of Directors

On the other end of the spectrum from paper or rubberstamp Boards are Boards of Directors with true decision making and oversight powers which are used to:

- ✓ Set the overall strategy of the company
- ✓ Oversee the performance of the management of the company without replicating management activities but with sufficient resources to be able to challenge decisions and actions by management and family members

- ✓ Ensure appropriate Corporate Governance structure is in place by insisting on sufficient disclosure levels, adequate minority shareholder protection mechanisms and generally promoting a robust control environment
- ✓ Secure senior management succession
- ✓ Ensure availability of financial resources to allow pursuit of the strategy
- ✓ Ensure adequate internal controls and Risk Management
- ✓ Report to the owners and other interested parties, including regulatory and tax authorities.

The size and composition of a Board of Directors has a major influence on its ability to carry out the role outlined above. Too big and it can become unwieldy, costly and difficult to act in a collegial way. Too small and it risks not having sufficient breadth of experience and skills to carry out its role well. Whilst there is no strict limit on size a manageable size is usually seven to eleven members with the actual number inevitably also driven by the complexity and scale of the underlying business. It is highly desirable that directors as a group have broad but identifiable set of skills and experiences in the areas of the Board's competence and authority, including General Management, Strategy Formulation, Finance, Accounting, Risk Management, Marketing and Operations. In this context, it is advisable to select individual Board directors both for the value add they can add as individuals and the ways they complement the rest of the Board.

3.4.1.4. Spectrum of oversight body choices for family-controlled business

We have already encountered different types of family-controlled businesses and different types of oversight bodies. It is natural that Corporate Governance arrangements, including the nature of the oversight bodies that are implemented, will be influenced by the nature of ownership of the family-controlled business, as we have encountered in Chapter 3.1. If listed, then their Corporate Governance arrangements will be dictated by the listing requirements of the particular stock exchange on which they are listed. Typically, a family-controlled company that is listed will have a strongly independent Board of Directors that will include independent, non-family members and sometimes even chaired by a non-family member.

When the company is owned 100% by the family, the Corporate Governance arrangements of the company are a matter entirely for the family itself. The existence and role of the Board of Directors will be at the discretion of the family. If a Board exists, participation of non-family members will also be at the discretion of the family. And in many cases, such family-only Boards will be paper or rubberstamp Boards intentionally limited to ensuring legal and regulatory compliance. On the other hand, if there are external parties with a shareholding in the company, however small their shareholding is, the Corporate Governance arrangements of the company are also of great interest to these external parties. Indeed, if there are external parties as minority shareholders, one of the key aspects of Corporate Governance will be the protection of their rights as shareholders. In such cases, the companies usually have Boards which include at least one non-family member and at least some responsibility to ensure protection of minority shareholder rights.

Beyond the private vs. public ownership dimension, another key characteristic that influences the Corporate Governance arrangements of a family-controlled business, especially when the company is privately-held, is the generation of the family that controls the company. Along this dimension, firstly there are family businesses which are controlled by their founder. Irrespective of their size, the total control usually exercised by the founder both in ownership and management terms influence everything in the business, including its governance. But the founder who is also the sole or controlling shareholder is usually not answerable to anyone. Boards of Directors for such founder-dominated companies, tend to be more advisory in nature (Advisory Board) or driven mainly by the need to comply with prevailing laws and regulations (paper or rubberstamp Board).

Secondly, there are family businesses which are controlled and managed by the children of the founder in a "sibling partnership" arrangement. Irrespective of their size, the participation of at least two individuals in the ownership and management of the business means that at the very least arrangements are required to govern how these individuals interact with each other and share and exercise control over the business. A company controlled by two or more founders can be considered a variant of this sibling partnership type of family business.

Thirdly, there are family businesses whose longevity means their ownership is spread amongst multiple family members that extend to a third generation, such as cousins who are grandchildren of the original founder. These businesses are often described as a "cousins confederation" and the fact the ownership and control is more dispersed means they also require yet more complex governance arrangements than the sibling partnership type of family businesses. In fact, at this stage of evolution, a family business is in effect indistinguishable from businesses which are not controlled by a family with respect to what are appropriate Corporate Governance arrangements. Indeed, it is the introduction of Corporate Governance at this stage of evolution of ownership in the family business, that promotes and enhances the prospects of the business remaining under family control beyond the third generation.

As the diagram below illustrates, the Corporate Governance arrangements of the family business are heavily influenced by its ownership structure and the generation of the family that controls it. The size and complexity of the underlying business also plays a very significant role in the design of Corporate Governance arrangements.

Figure 3.4.1.4.a. Corporate Governance in Family Businesses

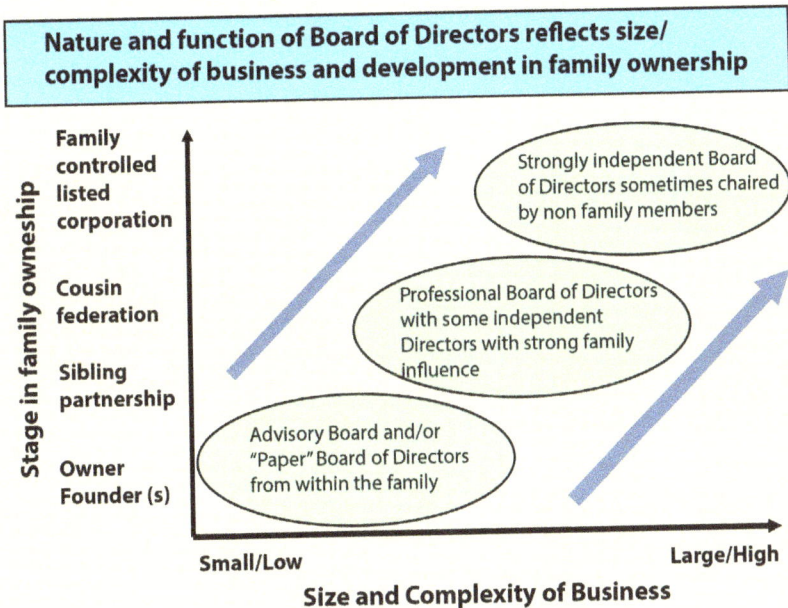

It may appear that choosing what type of oversight body to introduce into their business is one the most important one-time decisions a family or founder controlling a business has to make. Whilst it is indeed important to match the type of oversight body of a family business with the ownership structure, family generation in charge and the size and complexity of the business, since none of these factors stays constant over time, the match also evolves over time. Instead of a one-time decision, the founder or controlling family are in fact faced with the challenge of ensuring the evolution of their company's oversight arrangements.

3.5. Effective oversight in a family-controlled business

Effective oversight is desirable for any business and family-controlled businesses are no exception. Thus the first two elements for achieving effective oversight in a family-controlled business are the same as in any other business, namely:

a. An appropriate oversight structure with an oversight body (e.g. a Supervisory Board, an Advisory Board or a Board of Directors) whose role and function is fit for purpose; and

b. Members of the oversight body who individually and collectively are effective and ensure the oversight body itself is carrying out its duties and responsibilities.

Beyond these two ingredients, which are necessary for any business, there is a third element that needs to be taken into account in composing the oversight body of a family-controlled business. This is the interaction of the oversight Board members with the family itself.

3.5.1. Effective Board of Directors in a family-controlled business

The quest for effective oversight is common in both family and non-family businesses. Thus, it is instructive to look at what constitutes an effective Board of Directors in any business to begin with and then layer the requirement of effectiveness in a family ownership setting. Clearly, there are certain key ingredients that contribute to the effectiveness of a collective oversight body like a Board of Directors. In order to identify them, it is helpful to consider the following:

✓ What makes an individual director an effective director?

✓ What makes a Board of Directors effective as a collective body?

✓ How can one analyze the competence of an individual director and that of a Board of Directors?

Then armed with an understanding of what ingredients improve the prospects of an effective Board of Directors, we can examine how family ownership can influence these ingredients.

3.5.1.1. Individual Board Director's effectiveness

A Director's Duties and Responsibilities

Being a director of a company means having duties and responsibilities, otherwise it would be an empty title. The duties can be broadly categorised as Duty of Care and Duty of Loyalty.

Under Duty of Care, a director must ensure that prior to making a decision, he or she must act in a reasonable manner and make a good faith effort to analyze and consider all relevant information available for their consideration. They must act with diligence and competence, attend Board meetings regularly, be prepared for them and actively participate in them. Ultimately, they must make decisions on an informed and deliberative basis.

Under the Duty of Loyalty, directors must ensure that in performing their duties, they must be loyal to the company, putting this loyalty ahead of any other interests. In this context, there should be immediate disclosure to the rest of the Board of any conflicts or potential conflicts of interest arising in any matter that is affecting the Company and the Board. And where the Board is asked to decide on matters that could involve an actual or potential conflict of interest, the director affected by such a conflict should abstain from voting.

There are also legal responsibilities that arise in law. In law, directors are personally responsible and sometimes personally liable for the company's compliance with financial, tax, environmental, health and safety regulatory requirements.

Figure 3.5.1.1.a. Duties and Responsibilities of a Director

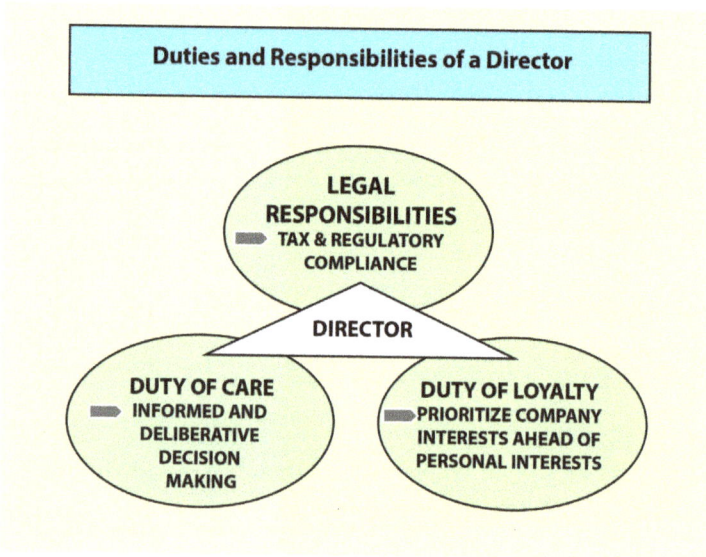

Desirable Board Director competencies

A Board director's effectiveness is driven by competence along four key dimensions:

✓ Governance knowledge – essential governance knowledge and understanding that all directors should posses or develop in order to be effective Board members

✓ Behavioural attributes and competencies – attributes and competencies that enable individual Board members to use their knowledge and skills to function well as team members and to interact with key stakeholders, plus the values and beliefs that are compatible with those of the organization.

✓ Technical or professional knowledge – technical or professional skills and specialist knowledge in specific disciplines (e.g. skills and knowledge in general management, finance, marketing, accounting, human resources) that can assist with ongoing aspects of the Board's role

✓ Industry knowledge – experience in and knowledge of the industry in which the organization operates

Figure 3.5.5.1.b. Desirable competencies for an effective Director

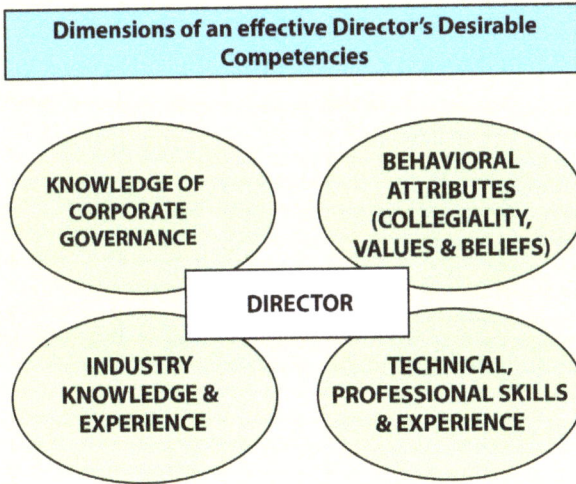

And the level of competence of a Board director reflects a combination of factors:

- ✓ Experience – Relevant prior experience in management, industry and in Board roles
- ✓ Knowledge – Relevant knowledge of the organization and/or its markets
- ✓ Skills – Functional knowhow in areas that are important for the business and its oversight by the Board (e.g. accounting, finance, risk, marketing, human resources, legal, etc.)
- ✓ Attitudes – Approach to collegial working of Board
- ✓ Values and Beliefs – Compatibility with company's ethics and integrity

At a minimum a Board director should be expected to have

- ✓ Grasp of governance basics – Familiarity with director's individual duties and responsibilities as a director of the organization is absolutely essential. It is self-evident that if they do not have a grasp of their own duties and responsibilities, directors are very unlikely they will discharge them effectively
- ✓ Basic financial and legal literacy – Ability to understand basic financials and familiarity with basic legal framework regulating companies and directors' responsibilities are also very important. Once again if

they are not able to understand basic financial concepts and reports, then they will be less effective in acting as part of an oversight body

✓ Compatibility with company's ethics and values – Directors are in essence ambassadors to stakeholders and they need to practice and embody the ethics and values of the organization. Any incongruent comments or behaviour from a director can affect the organization's reputation with serious consequences.

✓ Capacity for teamwork whilst remaining one's own person – The Board can become dysfunctional if directors are not able to act in a collegial manner but equally, a director must be prepared to voice their own views and not be cowed by peer pressure and allow the Board to succumb to group think.

3.5.1.2. Board of Director's effectiveness

The effectiveness of a Board of Directors is usually a function of

✓ The composition of the Board – Directors as a group need to have broad but identifiable sets of skills and experiences in the areas of the Board's competence and authority including Strategy Formulation, Finance, Accounting, Risk Management, Marketing, General Management, etc. They also need to be effective as a group, hence the group chemistry and dynamic is an important parameter in this dimension

✓ The competence of the directors – Individual directors need to have demonstrable skills and experience that allow them to complement the group and also add value as individuals

✓ The size of the Board – Too small for a complex business and it will not provide the oversight needed and too big for a small organization and it will become wasteful and potentially dysfunctional. Whilst no strict limit of size can be prescribed in a one size fits all approach, the size needs to be manageable and be determined so as to facilitate communications and decision-making.

✓ The commitment of the directors – Directors both individually and as a group need to invest the time and effort to ensure they are engaging in properly informed and deliberative decision-making.

Experience and empirical evidence shows that high performing Boards share

✓ Clarity regarding role and focus – they do not get drawn into management issues but focus instead on their oversight role

✓ An effective Chairman – a Chairman sets the tone of the Board discussions and the Board's interaction with the company's senior management. An effective Chairman is a master at managing these interactions and in ensuring the Board remains capable to discharging its duties to the fullest extend

✓ A balanced Board team where there is multiplicity of viewpoints and experiences which can inform the deliberations of the Board. In this way the risk the Board gets blindsided is reduced.

✓ A Board culture of trust and respect where the Directors genuinely recognize they are part of a collective oversight body and behave accordingly towards each other.

And effective Board members exhibit the following attributes:

✓ They are prepared and keep commitments and they are fully engaged and focused on their duties and responsibilities

✓ They speak their minds – They speak openly and with no fear and can deliver hard or uncomfortable truths constructively

✓ They build independent relationships – They get to know each other and key management personnel and meet with and talk to each other and key management personnel outside meetings. This allows them to be better informed which can lead to better decision-making

✓ They are resources rich – They bring a breadth of experience and have the capacity to continue to add value over time

✓ They are strategically engaged but operationally distant – Whilst sufficiently familiar with operational matters to inform strategic view they do not interfere with actual management

3.5.1.3. Competence matrix analytical tool

Analyzing the competence of individual Board members requires first of all the identification of the skills and competences along which each director is to be assessed. These skills and competencies must be relevant to the business and the function of the Board. The list of these skills and competencies will vary from company to company but as we have discussed already in the preceding section, there are some competencies that are highly desirable in a Board Director. So, even across different industries, the list of skills and competencies is likely to include the ones already encountered in the preceding section (e.g. industry knowledge, functional and technical skills and experiences, etc.) as well as other ones that will address issues of balance and diversity (e.g. age, gender). Once the dimensions have been identified, individual directors' profiles can be constructed in a matrix-like manner and at a level of granularity that is informative and helpful. Such a competence matrix can be further elaborated, if so desired, with different weights for the different dimensions. As can be seen from the illustrative example below, even a simple competence matrix can be a very information rich tool.

Figure 3.5.1.3.a. Director Competence Matrix
Analytical Tool – individual director

Director Competence Matrix as analytical tool for individual Board director profile assessment			
ILLUSTRATIVE EXAMPLE			
Skill/Competence	Director 1	Director 2	Director 3	Candidate 1
General Management Experience	High	Low	Medium	High
Leadership	High	Medium	Medium	Medium
Finance & Audit	Low	Medium	Low	High
Company Knowledge	High	High	Medium	Low
Age diversity	45	30	55	45

Director Competence Matrix can bring out, including in visual manner, the relative strengths of individual board members and board candidates

Rating individual directors in relation to skills and competencies through the use of a competence matrix, highlights in a systematic way the areas of relative strength and areas for further development for each individual Board member. In the case of rating candidate directors, the use of a competence matrix tool can help assess whether and how individual prospective new directors can help balance the Board's set of skills and competencies

The competence matrix tool can also be used at the collective Board level as illustrated in the diagram below.

Figure 3.5.1.3.b. Director Competence Matrix
Analytical Tool – Board assessment

Director Competence Matrix Tool for collective Board assessment			
ILLUSTRATIVE EXAMPLE			
Skill/Competence	**Level of Importance**	**Current Board Representation**	**Recruitment Priority**
General Management Experience	High	Medium	Medium
Leadership	High	Medium	Medium
Finance & Audit	High	Low	High
Age diversity	Low	High	Low

In this illustrative example it is highly desirable for the next Board member to be recruited to have strong skills & experience in Finance & Audit

As can be seen from the example above, combined ratings of all existing directors can provide insight on the balance of skills and competencies existing on the Board and highlight priority areas that need to be covered, possibly with recruitment of additional, new directors.

3.5.2. Interaction of oversight body with controlling family

Having examined what makes an individual director effective and what renders a Board of Directors effective in a Corporate Governance sense, it is important to examine whether and how the interaction of the oversight body in a family business with the controlling family, can affect the effectiveness of their oversight. The simple answer is that unlike non-family businesses where shareholding tends to be diffuse and directors are answerable to every shareholder and no individual shareholder in particular, in family-controlled businesses, the controlling family will very often have a presence on the Board and the non-family directors are having to deal with fellow directors who are also significant shareholders. This duality of the role of family directors affects the whole dynamic of the Board of a family-controlled business. The Competence

Matrix tool can easily be cast aside in a Family First family business and family members can become directors simply because they are family members without any or much discernible value-add to bring to the workings of the Board or the underlying business. In such situations non-family Board members need to have the relevant skills and experience to compensate for the family members who bring few or none of their own. Conversely, in a Business First family business, the competence matrix tool might be used first within the family members to determine who from their rank is best qualified and suited to join the family business Board and the family may consciously ensure a minimum number of non-family members are present on the Board.

Fundamentally, the key question is whether the controlling family respects and recognizes the value of having independent, non-family members on the Board of their family business. Those that do not value independence in their directors, will tend to appoint family friends and trusted management insiders rather than truly independent non-family members. It then depends even more on how much skill and integrity these friendly Board members can discharge their duties with, in order to protect both the business and the controlling family from the types of abuses that we have encountered earlier in this chapter. The role of such insiders can easily slip into having to be the conscience and compass of the Board against the worst impulses of family Board members. When such insiders fail to be an effective check and balance mechanism, disaster can strike for both family and business.

The value and significance of the presence of independent, non-family Board members in the prosperity and longevity of family businesses has also been confirmed in various studies. A US study of more than 80 family-owned businesses run by third or later generations, showed the existence of an active and outside (i.e. non-family-controlled) Board was the most important distinguishing characteristic and critically important element in the survival and success of these companies.

Thus, families that wish to see their family businesses prosper and pass onto future generations are well advised to take a Business First approach and seek out independent directors for their Boards and then allow such independent directors to add value through good Corporate Governance. The advantages of having independent directors are manifold and controlling families should avoid blunting these advantages by forgetting to respect and value the independence of non-family Board members. These advantages include

- ✓ Bringing an outside perspective on strategy and control
- ✓ Adding new skills and knowledge that might not be available within the firm or the family
- ✓ Bringing an independent and objective view which is not driven by the family
- ✓ Making hiring and promotion decisions independent of family ties
- ✓ Acting as a balancing element between the different members of the family and sometimes as a "buffer" and/or objective judges of disagreements among family-member managers
- ✓ Benefitting from their business and other contacts and connections
- ✓ Focusing Board meetings on business matters and discouraging family issues influencing business decision-making

3.6. Chapter closing thoughts

Family business play a vibrant and dynamic role in market economies. But only one in three make it to the second generation and only about one in eight make it to the third generation. Paradoxically, families which adopt a Family First approach in the governance arrangements and management of their family business damage the prospect of longevity for their family business. Conversely, families willing to prioritize the needs of the business ahead of the needs of family members, safeguard and enhance the prospects of longevity for their family business. The discipline that families need to utilize in dealing with this paradox, where putting family interests first actually harms those interests in the long term in respect of the family business, is Family Governance and is the subject of the next Chapter.

Chapter 4:
Family Governance

4.1. Definition, importance and introduction of Family Governance

What is Family Governance?

The structure, policies and processes which are used to govern the interactions of the family members between themselves as well as with the family business in a fair and transparent way constitute the discipline of Family Governance.

Family Governance starts with a **Family Constitution or Charter** which articulates the family vision, mission values and policies regulating the family members' relationship with the business. This is implemented via institutions with different forms and specific roles which include

- ✓ The **Family Assembly** – The Family Assembly sets the vision and approves major family related policies and procedures and elects the Family Council
- ✓ The **Family Council** – The Family Council is in effect the Board of the Family. It manages the interaction of the family with the family business, resolves conflicts and it develops major family related policies
- ✓ **Family Committees** – Family Committees are committees made up of family members with specific responsibilities (e.g. family office, education, preparation of next generation of business leaders)
- ✓ The **Family Office** – The Family Office is tasked with the management of the family's wealth outside their interest in the family business and its organization can include family members as well as professionals with relevant experience and expertise who are not family members

Figure 4.1.a. Simple Family Governance structure

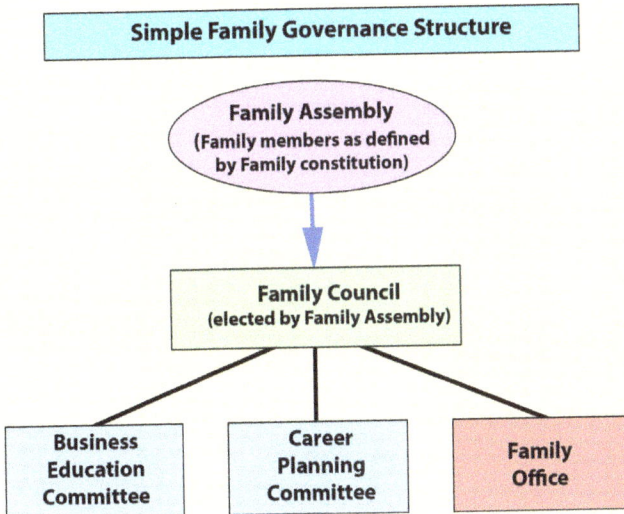

Why does Family Governance matter?

Family members play a range of roles in the governance of their business. As a result there are interactions between the business and the family and different family members at multiple levels. These interactions pose specific challenges and risks that need to be regulated in a transparent way. If these challenges and risks are not addressed, they can undermine the longevity of the family business. At its core, Family Governance seeks to firstly promote family harmony and through the creation of a predictable and transparent framework governing the family's interaction with the business, also promote and oversee the sustainable development of the family business.

Multigenerational family businesses with great longevity share certain attributes which suggest these characterize a well-functioning family governance structure

- ✓ Communicating the family values, mission and long-term vision to all the family members
- ✓ Keeping family members (especially those not active in the business) informed about major business successes, challenges and strategic direction
- ✓ Communicating the rules and decisions that might affect the family members' employment, dividends and other benefits they usually get from the business
- ✓ Establishing formal communication channels that allow family members to share their ideas, aspirations and issues
- ✓ Allowing the family to come together and make any necessary decisions

Well-functioning Family Governance builds trust amongst family members (inside and outside the business) and unifies the family, thus improving the long-term viability prospects of the family business.

For a simple checklist on the status of Family Governance in a family business please see Annex 3: Family Governance Summary Checklist.

4.2. Constituent elements of Family Governance

Family Governance can be informal or formal depending on the preferences of the family. When informal, the person acknowledged as the family leader, patriarch or matriarch, tends to drive or make decisions. Policies and committees are formed on ad hoc basis and may change over time as conditions change.

When Family Governance becomes more formalized, it is normally based on a set of principles agreed by the family members and which are captured in a formal way in a Family Constitution. The Family Constitution will usually outline the Family Institutions (e.g. Family General Assembly, Family Council, Family Office, Family Committees etc.) which comprise and give substance to the concept of Family Governance. The Constitution will also lay down the rules of membership and decision-making for these institutions as well as their scope of competence and authority. It will also contain certain key Family Policies and provide for a mechanism for these to evolve over time as well as for the introduction of new policies as the need arises. Finally, like any other constitution, it should include the rules by which the constitution itself can evolve over time. We review these constituent elements of Family Governance in the sections below.

4.2.1. The Family Constitution

4.2.1.1. What is a Family Constitution and how does it help?

What is a Family Constitution?

A Family Constitution documents the values and principles that will underpin the conduct of the family business. It defines the strategic objectives of the business and sets out the way in which the family will make decisions affecting the ownership and management of the business.

Though it cannot circumvent or avoid family conflict over the family business, it can provide for a mechanism by which conflict can be successfully managed and resolved. Indeed, even the very process of creating a constitution forces the family to consider important issues about the future of the family business, including potential future conflict between the family members and how to resolve such conflict, that might otherwise not be considered and thus leave the family unprepared when such conflict situations arise.

Common Areas addressed by family constitutions

Common areas addressed by family constitutions include:

- ✓ Strategic business objectives reflecting agreed family values and aspirations for the business
- ✓ The process for hiring, assessing and remunerating family members employed in the business
- ✓ The rules for nominating, training, assessing and appointing management successors
- ✓ Processes for nominating and assessing individuals for appointment to the family company's Board of Directors or family council (or equivalent) if one exists
- ✓ The composition and rules of conduct for a Family Council or equivalent body, which acts as an executive and coordinating body of the affairs of the family and as its conduit for the family's interaction with the family business

✓ Communication and disclosure policies between company and family

✓ The process for resolving conflicts about the business between members of the family

✓ The rights and obligations of shareholders in the family company

✓ Recommended or compulsory retirement age for family directors and managers

✓ Processes for buying out family shareholders in the business

✓ Policies concerning external, non-family ownership and management of the business

✓ Procedures for amendments to the constitution

How does a family constitution help?

As the family evolves and successive generations enter the business several changes occur. For example, the number of individuals with an ownership interest in the business increases. The expectations held by these individuals for the business begin to diverge. As the business expands, it makes increasing financial and management demands on its owners. Some members of the family may have greater and some lesser involvement or no involvement in the business, yet all may still retain an ownership interest in the family business. A family constitution helps the family deal with these changes constructively. Overall, a family constitution requires the family to think about important decisions before they have to be made and to find agreement on important family and business goals as well as on the process by which important decisions can be made even when the interests and views of individual family members may diverge.

4.2.1.2. When should a Family Constitution be adopted and what factors should influence it?

When should a constitution be adopted?

There is no set time when a Family Constitution has to be adopted. In practice, a Family Constitution is most likely to be adopted or revised at the time of generational change within the business. This could be when the business is about to be passed on from the founder to their children with two or more branches of the family becoming in charge of the business. Another transition which may trigger the adoption of a Family Constitution is the transition from second to third generation, which can further increase both the number of owners and the diversity of their ambitions for the business.

A generational change can be unplanned as a result of an unexpected demise of the existing proprietor. In light of that, and given that formulating a family constitution takes time and may require a number of family meetings, it is in fact wise for a Family Constitution to be drafted and agreed well ahead of an expected transition. In this way, even generational changes that are unplanned, can take place more smoothly.

Guiding Principles affecting a Family Constitution

Drafting a constitution requires agreement on some general guiding principles:

- ✓ What comes first, the family or the business? Perhaps a decision will be taken to retain and manage the business so that it can provide jobs and financial support for future generations of the family.
- ✓ Is ongoing family ownership and management in the best interests of the business?
- ✓ Is continuing ownership of the business likely to create tensions and divisions within the family?

When it comes to the family business, the Family Constitution needs to reflect the family's objectives for the business:

- ✓ Will we continue to grow and develop the business?
- ✓ Will we maintain family ownership?
- ✓ Will we seek to increase the strength of the family entity?

Influence of family objectives on Family Constitution

The family's objectives for the business, which are captured by the guiding principles that influence the Family Constitution, also influence the policies and procedures that the Family Constitution will have to include. As we can see from the three most common family objectives below, for any objective and purpose articulated, there will need to be appropriate policies and procedures provided for in the Family

Constitution in order to enhance the prospects of achieving the articulated objective and purpose.

If one of the main objectives of the family in adopting a Family Constitution is to ensure continued development of the family business, then the Family Constitution will need to include among others policies and procedures for:

- ✓ Assessing the skills and frameworks needed at Board and management level to ensure that the best resources are available to facilitate the continued development of the business
- ✓ Agreeing ground rules for the planning of the succession of the business' leadership
- ✓ Clearly defining business and family governance issues and their resolution

If one of the main objectives of the family in adopting a Family Constitution is to bolster the strength and harmony of the family, then the Family Constitution will need to include among others:

- ✓ Processes to establish and review unifying family values and vision for the business.
- ✓ Mechanisms for the family to get together and exchange information in relation to the business
- ✓ Policies for making resources or services available to the broader family
- ✓ Ground rules for assessing and selecting family members to join the business
- ✓ Rules delineating family and business issues

If the main objective of the family in adopting a Family Constitution is to facilitate the continued family ownership of the business, then policies to be considered for inclusion in the Family Constitution will include among others:

- ✓ Policies for the interfamily transfer or sale of shares
- ✓ Dividend policies
- ✓ Policies in relation to the timing, participation and quantum of liquidity events

✓ Policies setting out the methods of communication of information to shareholders

✓ Policies in relation to the representation of shareholders at Board level and shareholder meetings

✓ Policies for the nomination and assessment of directors

✓ Policies setting out the behaviours of, and the relationships between shareholders

✓ Policies for resolving conflicts

Figure 4.2.1.2.a. Influence of Family's purpose on Family Constitution

Influence of Family's purpose on Family Constitution	
PURPOSE	**POLICIES & PROCEDURES TO BE CONSIDERED**
Continued development of the business	• Mobilization of resources to faciliate continued development of the business • Succession planning • Delineation of family and business issues and regulation of family and business interactions
Bolster Family Strength and Harmony	• Establish family values and vision for the business • Exchange of information and selection of family's representatives inside the business • Sharing of resources to family outside the business • Delineation of family and business issues and regulation of family and business interactions
Facilitate continued family ownership of the business	• Dividend policies, interfamily share sales/transfers, liquidity events • Representation at Board, Shareholders' Meeting & Exchange of information between family inside and outside the business • Seleciton and assessment of directors • Relationships between shareholders and conflict resolution

4.2.1.3. How does a family introduce a Family Constitution?

As illustrated in the diagram below, introducing a Family Constitution is a process with specific steps and milestones.

Figure 4.2.1.3.a. The process of introducing a Family Constitution

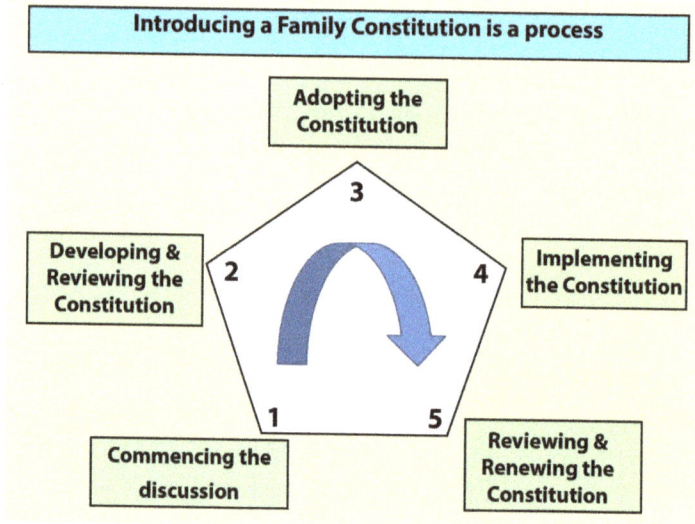

In each stage of the process, there needs to be a clearly articulated purpose and consideration given to who will lead the effort and how family members will engage with the process.

In commencing the discussion, there are three main purposes to be addressed. Firstly, there is a need to raise awareness within the family and raise support from the family for the need for a Family Constitution. This need extends to educating the family as to the need to adopt a set of guidelines to unify and codify the family's values and decisions on matters before they arise. This stage of the effort can be led by an experienced and trusted external advisor or a trusted non-family director and one of the family leaders. Without the involvement of at least one family leader, the exercise will not gain the legitimacy to advance. The family can be engaged by invitation as the persons leading the effort begin to circulate articles about families in crises as well as successful long term, multigenerational family businesses. The key message from the persons leading the exercise to the family members should be unambiguous – Family Governance is the hallmark of successful multigenerational family businesses and the absence of Family Governance is associated with declining family fortunes and extinct family businesses.

Secondly, there is a need to decide which family members will be involved in the process and who will chair it. In deciding who is best placed to chair the process, the family needs to first determine if their orientation will be family first or business first. If the family's interests are to be preeminent, then a family member, usually one respected by all family members will need to chair the process, irrespective of their current ties and role to the business. On the other hand, if the interests and needs of the business are to be preeminent, then it could be a family member who is the CEO or Chairman of the company that chairs the process. Smaller families may choose to involve all stakeholders in the discussions. For example a founder with adult, unmarried children, may decide to involve them all plus his/her spouse. In larger families or multibranch families, participation in the process may be via selection or nomination or through volunteering. Whichever way a family decides to go, it is important to consider a mix of generations and a mix of family members working in the business and family members not involved in the business, as well as those who hold current ownership interests and those who don't but are expected or will be allowed to do so in future. Finally, there is a need to agree on the decision-making process. A family's leader needs to steer the discussions and ensure a consensus is reached but the family can also engage a trusted external advisor to facilitate reaching consensus.

The next big phase after the discussion phase is the Development and Review phase. This phase can be pursued through a project team approach, whereby certain people are charged with working on the matter and reporting back to the family group, or a committee approach, whereby there will be a schedule of meetings and topics where all participants are involved. If it is a project approach, then an external consultant or advisor could be charged with leading the effort and be accountable to the family council and to the family project team so that progress can be discussed and monitored. If it is a committee approach, the family can determine its committee to work on the process and set a schedule of meetings and discussion topics and appoint a specific family member to document discussions held and decisions made. This family committee may find it useful to appoint an external facilitator or advisor to assist with the process. Under a committee approach, as in the Discussion Phase, the leadership responsibility for this phase depends on the orientation the family wishes to adopt. If it's a Business First approach, the CEO or

Chairman of the family business could have the responsibility of leading this phase. If it's a Family First approach, the family council or one nominated family member will assume the leadership responsibility.

The next step in the process involves adopting the Family Constitution. This step requires agreement on the decision-making and overall approval process and needs to cover who can vote, and how voting will take place and decisions made. An external consultant or advisor can help lead this phase and be accountable to the family council. As in the previous phases, the leadership responsibility will be assumed by the CEO or Chairman or another member of the family depending on the family's intended orientation of the family business. It is common for a Family Constitution to be approved and ratified by the family members based on their level of ownership, particularly on matters that concern ownership of the business. It is also common for parts of a Family Constitution to be adopted on a per capita basis rather than ownership interests and these parts are usually concerned with the family's values and its role in the management of the business.

Implementing the Family Constitution once it has been adopted by the family is the most crucial part of the process. It requires significant time and commitment from the family and the sharing and airing of concerns and aspirations. The importance of implementation once the constitution has been adopted cannot be emphasized enough. If the constitution is adopted but is not implemented, then the family and non-family management may question the family's commitment to it and grow both frustrated and reluctant to invest any more time on these matters in the future, which may lead to family disharmony. As in the previous phases, the leadership responsibility can be taken up by the CEO or Chairman where the business is to come first, or a respected family member from outside the business if the family is to come first. The family's involvement becomes more specific and formal as relevant documents are executed. The corporate documents (e.g. memorandum and articles of association) of the family business may have to be revised. Beyond executing documents, the family will also need to establish the structures and processes provided for in the Family Constitution it has adopted. For example, creating the family council if one was not already in existence, or formalizing its rules of engagement if one existed without clear terms of reference. There could also be appointments to the family business Board to be considered and filled as well as codifying and implementing agreed ground rules for succession planning. Once at this phase, any matter concerning the family or the family business that arises which has been considered and addressed by the constitution, should be dealt with based on the pre-agreed rules included in the constitution. As in any other implementation phase, the family should agree and adhere to agreed milestones and key dates in relation to implementation. Leading the efforts for the implementation phase can be the Family Council, or the CEO or even the Board of the family business. By communicating and performing agreed actions, the family and the business may sense greater accountability, professionalism and commitment.

Like any other type of constitution, it is impossible for a Family Constitution adopted at a specific point in time to remain unaltered forever. It is inevitable that conditions and circumstances of both the family and the family business will change over time along with the external conditions affecting both. It is therefore imperative that a Family Constitution provides within it the mechanisms for its periodic review and renewal that will allow successive generations to reaffirm what remains relevant and important, modify elements that need updating to reflect changing conditions and introduce new elements for important issues that had not existed before. The purpose of such periodic reviews is to ensure the constitution continues to address the concerns and needs of the family and the family business. The document should be a living document and be periodically finetuned to ensure it continues to be relevant and capable of being consistently applied. Such reviews can be scheduled according to set dates or at a minimum when a new generation joins the business. Major external trends and events can also be factors in deciding to hold a review and renew the Family Constitution. The responsibility for leading this phase can be with the Family Council or the CEO or the Board of the Company individually or on a shared basis.

4.2.1.4. Common pitfalls in constructing a Family Constitution

The most common pitfall families must be aware of is the absence of ground rules of how the process of constructing a Family Constitution will actually work. It may appear self-evident but it's still important to remember that nothing can be agreed if there are no ground rules on how decisions are made and agreements reached. So, ground rules are needed to help determine firstly, how should the decision-making process actually work. Specifically:

- ✓ Who is entitled to attend family meetings concerned with drafting of the Family Constitution
- ✓ Who should chair the family meetings
- ✓ What matters can be decided by a majority vote and what decisions will require unanimous agreement

Secondly, who should be responsible for translating the group's thinking and decisions into words on paper.

Another common pitfall is the process grinding to a halt at the first sign of disagreement on one or more elements of the proposed Family Constitution. Without a disciplined process of managing the agenda, a disagreement can fester and harden into conflict which becomes an obstacle to building consensus amongst the family. Thus, if contentious issues arise, it is wise to take such matters off the agenda temporarily, as this can help find consensus on other matters and limit the risk that the process becomes hostage to a small number of contentious issues.

A third pitfall is trying to rush the adoption of a Family Constitution. As is the case for any other document intended to provide guidance to present and future generations, it is important to allow plenty of time for consultation and decision-making so that participants will have a more considered view and become more deliberately engaged.

A fourth pitfall is to try and cover everything in fine detail from the first discussions or first draft or even the first version of a finally adopted Family Constitution. It is important to start with the general principles outlined and then work through to more detailed matters but recognize a constitution cannot cover all eventualities and as a living document will change and evolve over time as the family and the business does.

A fifth pitfall is for families thinking that later is better when it comes to starting the discussion on the need and principles of a Family Constitution. In fact, exactly the opposite is true given the need for consensus within the family in adopting such an important guiding document. The earlier generation that starts the process, the less dispersed the ownership and the more aligned the views and interests of the family members, who are usually fewer in numbers and more engaged in similar ways in the business, and hence reaching consensus is easier.

A final pitfall that can affect the process is the reliance on family members to drive the process without the involvement of any skilled external facilitators. Of course, it is possible the chosen family members are skilled themselves but the nature of the issues to be shepherded can make it difficult for a family insider to maintain the momentum, particularly if there is divergence of views and interests amongst different branches of the family. Thus, as good communication is vital for the process, some families can find it useful to involve a trusted non-family facilitator who can be catalytic in building consensus and be able to more easily raise issues that affect different branches of the family in ways that do not hinder the process.

4.2.2. The Family Institutions

As we have seen the Family Constitution sets out the Family Institutions and the scope of their competence and authority. The most indispensable of these are the Family Meeting, the Family Assembly and the Family Council. As described in the table below, the stage of evolution of the family business determines which of these is the vehicle through which the family influences the running of the family business. For example, families still being run by the founder patriarch or matriarch will usually and simply use informal family meetings to discuss the family business. On the other end of the evolution spectrum, a family business in the ownership of the third or later generations, will likely require a Family Council as the vehicle through which the family interacts with the family business.

Figure 4.2.2.a. Main Family Institutions

Main Family Institutions

	FAMILY MEETING	FAMILY ASSEMBLY	FAMILY COUNCIL
Stage	Founder(s)	Sibling partnership / Cousin Confederation	Sibling partnership / Cousin Confederation
Status	Usually informal	Formal	Formal
Membership	Usually open to all family members. Additional membership criteria may be set by the founder(s)	Usually open to all family members. Additional membership criteria may be set by the family	Family members elected by the Family Assembly. Selection criteria defined by the family
Size	Small size since family at founder(s) stage. Usually 6-12 members	Depend on the size of the family and membership criteria	Depends on criteria set up for membership. Ideally 5-9 members
Number of meetings	Depends on the stage of the business's development. When the business is growing fast, can be as frequent as once a week	1-2 times a year	2-6 times a year, usually in sync with underlying business board meetings
Main activities	Communication of family values and vision. Discussion and generation of new business ideas. Preparation of the next generation of business leader(s)	Discussion and communication of ideas, disagreements and vision. Approval of major family related policies and procedures. Education of family members on family business issues. Election of Family Council and other committees' members	Conflict resiolution. Development of the major family related policies. Planning. Education. Co-ordination of the work with the management and the Board and balancing the business and family dimensions

4.2.2.1. The Family Assembly

The Family Assembly or Family Forum is a formal forum for discussion for all family members about business and family issues. It brings family members together, usually twice a year, and facilitates dissemination of information about the business and airing of opinions on business development, thus reducing potential for conflict among family members. Typical issues handled include:

- ✓ Approval of any change in the family values and vision
- ✓ Education of family members about their rights and responsibilities
- ✓ Approval of family employment and compensation policies
- ✓ Election of family council members (if the council exists)
- ✓ Election of other family committees' members
- ✓ Other important family matters

Membership is usually open to all family members but some families set membership restrictions such as minimum age limits, limits to participation of in-laws, and voting rights during the assembly. Scheduling and chairing is usually by the family patriarch or matriarch or the family council.

4.2.2.2. The Family Council

The Family Council acts as the family's executive committee. It is elected by the Family Assembly, to deliberate and decide on family business issues and to act as a representative governance body for the Family Assembly in coordinating the interests of the family members in their business. The composition, structure and functioning of Family Councils varies but typical duties include

- ✓ Being the primary link between the family, the Board and the senior management
- ✓ Suggesting and discussing names of candidates for Board membership
- ✓ Drafting and revising family position papers on its vision, mission and values
- ✓ Drafting and revising family policies concerning the family business, such as family employment, compensation and family shareholding policies
- ✓ Dealing with other matters important to the family

Family councils usually comprise five to nine members and the Chairman is elected by the Family Assembly. Family council membership may be conditioned by age, experience and could be subject to term limits. Some families prescribe that their family council includes members from at least two generations to ensure different timeframes are considered in all decision-making and deliberations.

4.2.2.3. The Family Committees

As the name implies, Family Committees are formed by the family through the Family Council or the Family Assembly and are meant to deal with specific areas that are of interest to the family. Typical committees include among others:

- ✓ Education Committee
    - ✓ Responsible for nurturing the family's human capital and its capacity to participate in governance
    - ✓ Anticipates developmental needs of family members and organizes relevant events and activities (e.g. accounting seminar for family members)

- ✓ Career Planning Committee
    - ✓ Establishes and oversees entry policies for family members interested in joining the family business
    - ✓ Monitors careers of family members, offer career mentoring and keep shareholders and family council informed on family talent and its development

- ✓ Charities Committee
    - ✓ Coordinates and oversees the family's involvement with charities and philanthropy

- ✓ Shares Redemption Committee
    - ✓ Overseen by Family Council and arranges the sale of shares in the family business on behalf of family
    - ✓ May establish and manage a redemption fund for shareholders wishing to cash-in their shares at a fair price

- ✓ Family Reunion and Recreational Committee
    - ✓ Plans events and activities to nurture relationships between family members by providing opportunities to get together and enjoy each other's company

4.2.3. The Family Policies

Another building block in family governance which should be referenced, even if not spelled out in detail, in the Family Constitution, are the Family Policies, which can be developed by the Family Council and adopted by the Family Assembly. These are meant to provide the guidelines and in some respects the guardrails for the interaction of family members with the business and within the family. In this context, the number of policies formally adopted and the areas they seek to regulate will be driven by what the family considers as important at the time. This can of course change over time and existing policies can be updated or new ones introduced to deal with areas that become more important to the family over time. Typical areas for which families find it useful to adopt formal policies include among others:

- ✓ Family Employment policies – regulating how family members are employed in the family business (See Annex 3 for a sample of a set of Family Employment policies)
- ✓ Family Shareholding policies – regulating how family members' shareholdings in the family business can be transferred or sold
- ✓ Family Education policies – regulating how family members are supported in their education by the family or the family business (if it is education related to the business)
- ✓ Family Philanthropy policies – regulating how the family gets involved with charities and philanthropy
- ✓ Family Investment or Venturing policies – regulating how the family can support family members in investment and entrepreneurial activities outside the core family business

At least two sets of the above Policies, the Family Employment policies and the Family Shareholding Policies, are influenced by whether the family puts the Family's needs first or the Family Business's needs first. For example, Family Employment policies that are driven by a Family First viewpoint will make it easier for family members to be employed in the family business irrespective of actual need in the business and fit between family members' credentials and job requirements. Similarly, a Family First approach may make Family Shareholding policies extremely restrictive in terms of transfers to outsiders in order to retain full ownership and control of the family business within the family. So, just as there are no two families which are exactly alike, there is no particular policy or sets of policies that can be recommended for every family.

For example, with respect to the employment of family members by the family business, some families can use such member employment policies to act as a safeguard for the business and give priority to the needs of the business aiming to avoid ending up with surplus employees, particularly family member ones, and to avoid having employees who are unsuitable for the jobs they are given or to avoid keeping or expanding businesses simply in order to keep or create jobs for family members. In any event and in all circumstances, family employment policies should include the conditions of entry, staying and exiting from the business for the family members. They should also seek to ensure that the treatment of family employees relative to non-family employees is such that it promotes an atmosphere or fairness and motivation for all employees of the family business. Clearly, family employment policies need to be tailored to the specific needs of the family business and the circumstances of the family as "no one size fits all". Some families, often three or four generations after the founder founded the family business, preclude all family employment. Some families impose conditions that include minimum education level, prior work experience and age limits. (A sample Family Employment Policy is provided in Annex 4.)

In the case of Family Member Shareholding policies, there is usually a need to balance the needs of family members who will wish to sell their shares, i.e. seeking liquidity, and the interests of family members who are most concerned with ensuring the family retains control of the family business. Family Shareholding Policies can help set the right expectations among family members regarding shares' ownership rights and address issues such as:

- ✓ Can in-laws and other related family members own shares or not?
- ✓ Can shares be transferred freely within branches of the family?

A good shareholding policy also defines the mechanisms that allow family members to sell their shares if they prefer cash instead and will address issues such as:

- ✓ How are shares that are offered for sale offered to other family members who wish to buy these shares?
- ✓ How are prices for shares being sold to be computed?

Providing shareholders with a liquidity option for their shares, potentially through a Shares Redemption Fund financed from the underlying business profits, can help avoid conflicts.

4.2.4. The Family Office

4.2.4.1. What is a Family Office?

The management of wealth is a very substantial industry with specialized service providers for individuals and families with investable assets. These service providers include among others private banks, lawyers, accountants, fund managers and wealth managers. Such providers offer services to multiple clients and their value-add lies, at least in part, in their specialization and expertise in their respective fields. They are not exclusively focused on the wealth affairs of a particular client. When a family has substantial wealth, it often makes sense for the family to recruit a team that will look after the family's wealth affairs in a professional manner and on an exclusive basis. This team is usually called "The Family Office" and its principal activity is in allocating the family's wealth across asset classes and managers and in monitoring performance across asset classes and managers so appropriate adjustments to allocations can be made in a timely manner.

Figure 4.2.4.1.a. Family Office role within Family Governance

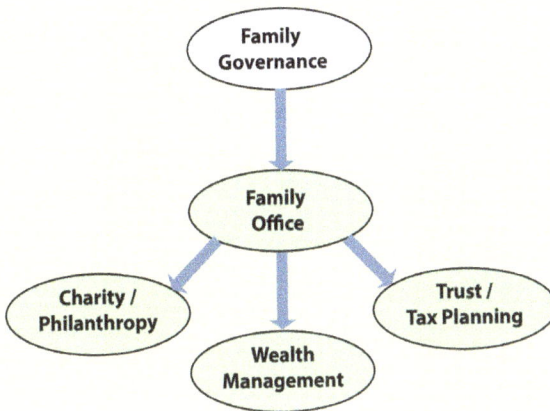

4.2.4.2. How does a Family Office help?

A Family Office helps in two major and distinct ways with the financial wellbeing of a family. Firstly, by housing the family's wealth in a separate structure and entrusting it to a qualified and professional team, which may include members of the family, the family ensures that the management and governance of the family's business or businesses are kept separate from the management of the wealth of the family. This is good for both the family-owned business and the family itself, since carrying out the two activities properly requires appropriate resources and focus and mixing the two risks compromising one or both. At the same time, such a separation does not mean that a Family Office cannot interact with the business of the particular family. Rather, the introduction of a Family Office to manage the wealth of the family, will usually mean that any interactions are more likely to be conducted and documented in a business-like manner and ideally on an arm's length basis. Experience shows that failures of family-controlled businesses are often linked with family owners treating business or corporate assets as personal or family assets, which constitutes a short-circuit of corporate and family governance. In this context, a Family Office is a circuit breaker that keeps a healthy distance between the business affairs of the family-controlled business and the wealth affairs of the family.

Secondly, a Family Office managed by a dedicated team with an exclusive focus on the wealth affairs of the family, can generate value for the family by finding an appropriate balance between keeping certain activities in-house and outsourcing others to specialized service providers. So, whilst a Family Office does not obviate the need to utilize specialized service providers, it does provide a capability and a muscle with which to drive better outcomes with such providers for the family.

4.2.4.3. How do you create a Family Office?

As has been mentioned, a Family Office focuses on managing the wealth of a family and therefore it requires a mix and balance of skills that will allow this to be done effectively and professionally. A team is usually recruited with relevant skills, experiences and networks, often from specialized service providers. Sometimes, members of the family with particular interest and strengths in allocating capital can be very active or even lead the Family Office on behalf of the entire family.

4.2.5. Professionalization of Management

4.2.5.1. What is Professionalization of Management?

The term is often associated with a family business transitioning from being run by a member or members of the founding family, i.e. owner-managers, to being managed by a team of professional managers who are not family members and therefore not part of the ownership structure of the business.

4.2.5.2. Why does Professionalization of Management matter?

Businesses with poor fundamentals usually do not last long, irrespective of the quality of their management. Businesses with good fundamentals can also falter if their management is not up to the task. Conversely, successful businesses achieving longevity are usually beneficiaries of good management. Thus, empirical evidence points to the management of a business being a crucial ingredient and determinant for its success and longevity. Getting the right management in place makes a difference. So, in circumstances where family members are no longer able or willing to act as managers, a business needs to transition to "professional" managers with no direct links to the owning family. Moreover, as a family's interests grow and diversify management challenges increase and family members may not be best suited for all aspects of management for all businesses under the family's control. Using non-family, professional managers can be a smart way to access a wider pool of talent and manage a larger and more complex business.

Figure 4.2.5.2.a. Professionalization of management in family businesses

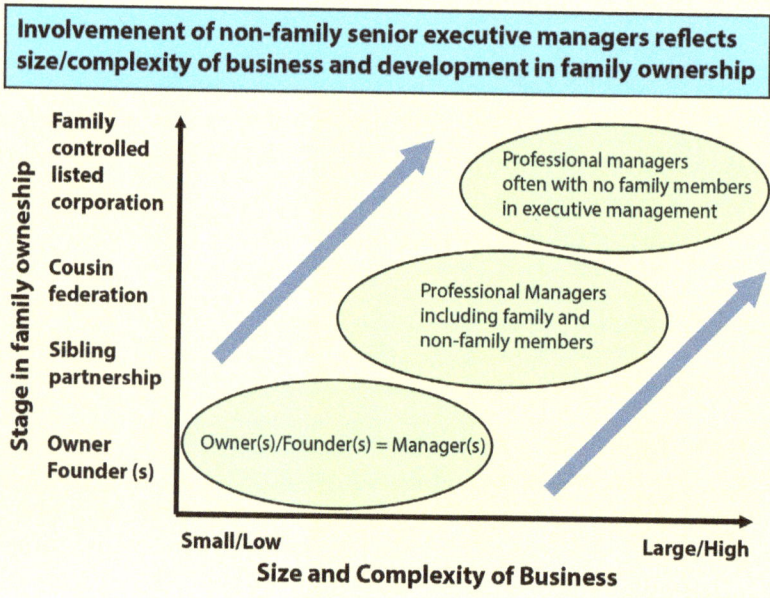

4.2.5.3. How is Professionalization of Management achieved?

Successful family businesses need succession plans in place in order to ensure smooth and timely transitions, whether from one family generation to the next or from the family owner-manager(s) to professional managers. Succession planning within the family or with the introduction of professional managers can sometimes be facilitated by external advisors.

4.2.6. Succession Planning in family business

It may be surprising to find succession planning being discussed as part of Family Governance and not as part of Corporate Governance. After all, it is an indisputable fact that transitions in senior leadership and management affect all companies. We consider that indeed succession planning is part of Corporate Governance but for family businesses, most often the key to successful succession planning lies with the family and therefore we feel it is important to consider it from the perspective of both the family and the business in the context of Family Governance instead of just as a matter of Corporate Governance.

As already mentioned, CEO and senior management succession is of crucial importance for all companies. Top managers are usually the drivers of a company's performance, growth and survival and therefore who is in charge, how their successors are selected and how the transition is managed can make a difference to the fortunes of any company. But management succession is even more important and potentially thorny for family businesses, particularly as the family grows larger. This is because as several potential senior management candidates become available from different branches of the family, conflicts may arise that may affect the company's performance and survival in its original form. It can sometimes also happen in the second generation, when siblings take over from a founder and they cannot decide who will take responsibility for what or which direction the family business should take. Putting off succession planning to last minute can lead to crises that can jeopardize the very survival of a family business as a multigenerational, multibranch family business. By contrast, timely CEO and senior management succession planning improves a family business's prospects for sustained performance and long-term survival. To use an analogy that every business owner can relate to, we all buy insurance before an event we worry about and not after the event has occurred. So, if the loss, incapacity or retirement of a CEO or senior manager stands to deprive the family business of leadership, experience and skills that are important to the future prospect of the business, leaving planning and decisions on succession to be taken after the loss or incapacity or retirement has occurred, is like buying fire insurance for a warehouse after the fire has burnt the warehouse. Succession planning is therefore to be done ahead of imminent and obvious need if it is to be considered timely.

Yet, succession planning in family businesses is often a topic that is avoided.

For example, family members may be delaying the discussion and decision of succession matters, in order to avoid potential frictions among family members in case several potential future CEOs, possibly from different branches of the family, are available within the family. Sometimes, family members may be delaying the decision because no current family member is seemed capable of replacing the current CEO. Family members may also be avoiding the succession issue in order not to discuss the topic of the eventual loss of a family leader and current CEO. Sometimes, the delays in succession planning reflect a current CEO's refusal to admit that the company can survive without them or is afraid of retirement. The risk from delays in succession planning, whichever way such delays arise, is that the company ends up with a CEO past their sell-by date and thrust into a crisis when they eventually step down. So whilst, timely succession planning for CEO or senior management has a positive effect on the prospects of a family business, delayed or no succession planning has a negative impact on the family business.

Beyond being timely, it is also vitally important that succession planning is formalized. A formal senior management succession plan ensures the skills and leadership necessary to replace any outgoing senior manager are available when needed. An effective CEO succession plan should allow for the selection of the most competent person (whether family or not) as next CEO. Moreover, an effective CEO succession plan should be inclusive of stakeholders and generate consensus in respect of the selected next CEO. Overall, a formalized succession plan ensures business continuity and thus increases the chances of survival of a family business as it is handed over from one generation to the next

A formal CEO succession plan means a structured approach with specific steps. The first of these steps is the recognition that a process of succession needs to essentially start as early as the current CEO is appointed. This is the only way to ensure continuity of the business and a carefully and well-prepared successor. To use a soccer analogy, every team that takes the field has a goalkeeper on the field of play and a goalkeeper on the substitutes bench just in case the goalkeeper on the field needs to be replaced. Similarly, every football team in the National Football League has a starting quarterback and a back-up quarterback who can replace the starting quarterback if needed and still execute the plays. So starting early is a very important aspect of a formal succession plan. In family businesses, it is especially advisable to start succession planning early, if the next CEO is expected to be chosen from within the family and would benefit from preparation and grooming. In most family businesses, it is the current CEO who initiates the succession planning process but the Board can also do so if current CEO is not initiating this early enough.

Another important step in a formal succession plan is the creation of career development systems for internal hires. If the next CEO is to come from within the family or the business, a rigorous career development system should be developed to prepare the potential CEOs and enhance their competence through any necessary education, training, rotation of responsibilities etc. Of course, such career development should be considered an ongoing activity in order to develop a pool of internal candidates for senior management positions, including CEO, at different age groups. This is true for most large non-family businesses as well.

A formal succession planning process is also a consultative process. The CEO should seek and get advice from external independent Board directors, if there are such directors on the Board, whilst narrowing the potential list of his/her internal successors. Similarly, the Family Council should be consulted, especially if the CEO candidate is from the family.

In addition, formal succession planning can facilitate the hiring from outside the business and the family when appropriate. For example, if no good internal candidates are available, the Nominations Committee of the Board of the family business can lead succession planning. In such circumstances, the hiring of an external CEO should be based on carefully defined criteria and in this context, Boards often find it useful to employ specialist executive search firms to get access to a wider pool of talent in recruiting an external CEO.

A formal succession planning process also provides an opportunity to build consensus around the selected candidate. This is vitally important since the success of a CEO in any company depends on their being accepted by key stakeholders in the company. For example an incoming CEO who has been selected through a rigorous selection process is much more likely to be accepted and be successful in their role than a favourite child of a founder who is parachuted to the top job with no real qualifications and credentials other than the family connection. Given the importance of such acceptance, it is always a good idea to involve all key stakeholders in a CEO selection process (i.e. Board of Directors, senior non-family managers, and family members).

Having started early, provided career development paths for internal candidates and mechanisms to consider external ones, the selection of a candidate being completed and accepted by the stakeholders, one could expect that as the process is 80% complete, as we would already have secured 80% of the benefit from succession planning. Unfortunately, transitions in leadership and senior management can work in a reverse 80/20 rule. Whereas normally the Pareto principle, commonly known as the 80/20 rule, holds that for many phenomena 80% of the result comes from 20% of the effort, with the implication that the last 20% of the benefit requires disproportionately more effort (the law of diminishing returns), in transitions we observe something different. Having followed a formal and disciplined succession planning process, a transition can still fail at the last step, which is the clarification and enforcement of the actual transition. This last step, which is typically and naturally tackled only once a new CEO has been selected, entails developing the transition paths for both the incoming CEO and the retiring CEO. Such transition paths should specify the transition date and also the levels of commitment expected from the retiring CEO (e.g. availability as an advisor to the incoming CEO, Board membership, etc.). The Board must enforce the transition paths, otherwise a retiring CEO who cannot let go and interferes with their successor's activities, can undermine the unity of senior management team and affect the prospects of the business. In such unfortunate scenarios, foregoing or messing up the last 20% of the effort risks failure of the transition altogether and foregoing any benefits from the 80% of the effort already invested in a formal succession planning process. Hence, the last 20% of the effort actually can secure most of the benefits from a formal succession planning process.

4.3. Problems arising in absence of Family Governance

Family Governance is intended to help family members deal with issues that affect both the business and the family from their perspective as owners of the business. It should therefore come as no surprise that the nature of the issues that become dominant in a family business are linked to the stage of evolution of the family business. Indeed, as summarized in the table below, the stage of development of the family business influence which shareholder issues become dominant in a family business and therefore present the main challenges that Family Governance arrangements are called to help resolve.

Figure 4.3.a. Shareholder issues in family businesses

Stages of ownership influence which shareholder issues become dominant in a family business	
Ownership stage	**Dominant Shareholder Issue**
Stage 1 : The Founder(s)	• Leadership transition • Succesion • Estate Planning
Stage 2 : The sibling partnership	• Maintaining teamwork and harmony • Sustaining family ownership • Succession
Stage 3 : The cousin confederation	• Allocation of corporate capital (e.g. dividends), debt and profit levels • Shareholder liquidity • Family participation and role in the family business (i.e. Board and executive management • Family linkage with the business from shareholder / partner perspective • Family mision and values • Resolution of any family conflict arising

The absence of Family Governance can leave issues like the ones summarized above unresolved and this in turn can lead to crises and risks for the business.

For example, imagine the case of a business which is controlled by an ageing founder who has not resolved to introduce or formalize any arrangements for their succession even though at least one or more of their children are clearly interested in and capable of taking over the running of the business.

➢ What happens if the founder becomes unable to continue with the business or worse still passes on without addressing the issue of succession?

➢ Does management of the business pass onto the eldest child?

➢ What if another child is also interested and perhaps even more capable or suitable to run the business?

➢ What if the siblings cannot agree on who should do what?

➢ Who will decide the succession in the absence of the founder and how will any disagreements amongst the siblings be resolved?

One can imagine siblings being able to reach agreements amicably on such important matters and both the business and the family continuing to prosper with the relationship between siblings remaining strong or even getting stronger. One can also imagine siblings not being able to agree and instead falling out with each other over the business and the business being eventually sold to a third party.

As another example, consider what happens to a family business which has survived the siblings partnership stage and is transitioning to a cousins confederation but without Family Governance in place. The same issues as mentioned above and more begin to require attention and resolution.

> ➢ How is succession to leadership positions to be handled? Is it based on merit or seniority of individual family members or level of ownership of the particular branch of the family?
> ➢ What is a reasonable split between dividends paid to family members (both active and nonactive in the business) and profits of the business that are redeployed in the business?
> ➢ How do family members get liquidity for their shares? What are the rules they have to observe if any, beyond relevant company law, if they want to reduce or increase their stake in the business? What restrictions do they face in terms of who they can sell to and how the sale price is determined?
> ➢ Do family members have a right to employment in the family business?
> ➢ How does the family resolve different views and priorities that different branches of the family may hold for the business?

You can imagine cousins and siblings being able to work out how to deal with such issues under the watchful eye of an influential founder still capable of reminding them of the beginning. But you can even more easily imagine cousins with competing and sometimes conflicting views, priorities and interests and in the absence of Family Governance, not being able to find consensual answers to such issues. In such circumstances, selling the family business can seem like a good compromise solution and is often the one action that garners most support amongst family members. The frequency with which third generation family businesses leave the founding family's control suggests this is a rather common occurrence. Indeed, only about one in eight of all family businesses make it past the third-generation stage.

4.3.1. The Steinberg and Gucci cases – lack of succession planning

Succession planning is the element of Family Governance which garners most attention, particularly when things go wrong and an explanation has to be found for the failure of a family business or its sale to new owners outside the family. Two cases in two entirely different sectors help illustrate how lack of succession planning or succession planning gone wrong can impact the fortunes of the family business and the family itself.

4.3.1.1. *The Steinberg supermarket store chain sale*

Steinberg's (renamed Steinberg in 1961) was a large family-owned Canadian grocery store chain that operated mainly in the province of Quebec and Ontario. The chain's origins were rather humble with the first grocery store being founded in 1917 in Montreal by the matriarch of the family, Ida Steinberg, a Hungarian immigrant. She believed quite correctly that giving each customer more than they had expected would lead to increased customer satisfaction and customer loyalty. Her five sons joined her in the business and one of them, Sam Steinberg proved to be an exceptional and visionary merchandiser. Under his leadership, Steinberg notched many firsts as it grew to become the largest supermarket chain in Quebec and then also expand into Ontario, including first to open an entirely self-service super-market and first to date fresh produce. When Sam Steinberg died suddenly of heart failure in 1978, the fortunes of the business began to falter. By that time the company was a listed company and Sam's branch of the family had a big enough stake to essentially control the company. But that required Sam's three daughters and their mother all voting together and unfortunately for a number of years they could not agree to do so. The family squabbles on who should lead the business and in which direction left the company at a disadvantage and in 1989 the business was sold for $1.3 billion to a consortium involving a shipping company with no experience in retail and the Caisse de dépôt et placement du Quebec, Quebec's pension-fund manager. By 1992, the name Steinberg disappeared from Canadian retailing.

The two main reasons often cited for the decline of the company's fortunes were the rising labour costs that resulted from the unionization that followed Sam's death and which placed the company's supermarkets at a competitive disadvantage with nonunionized competitors, and the lack of succession planning. In fact, what is most commonly understood by succession planning had seemingly been addressed years before Sam Steinberg had passed away, when he moved from being President of the company to being Chairman of the Board with his son-in-law Mel Dobrin becoming President in late 1969. Moreover, this handover had been accompanied with two other key executives, including a nephew and a non-family professional manager assuming Executive Vice President positions which resulted in apparently more decentralized decision-making. In the four years that followed this succession, the company's sales and share price doubled. So, if anything the changes that included succession in 1969 had seemed to work quite well. Yet the company and the family struggled when Sam Steinberg passed away nearly a decade later in 1978. Why?

A fly-on-the-wall Canadian documentary made in 1969 captured the discussions Sam Steinberg had with his 15 strong management committee over a three-day retreat on four key topics, including decision-making, professional management, succession and structure. This documentary, broadcasted in 1974 under the title "After Mr. Sam" is still available and quite instructive https://www.youtube.com/watch?v=2eqnhw2qzbs and the closing remarks by Sam Steinberg himself are perhaps the most telling of why, despite the succession it documented, Steinberg's decline after Sam Steinberg's death is attributed to lack of succession planning; in his words, "A company needs a driving force to move it forward and I am that driving force, always". Perhaps not surprisingly given how he had built the business over 50 years, despite appointing a new president and decentralizing decision-making to a degree by elevating his nephew and a non-family professional manager to Executive Vice President positions, Sam Steinberg continued to strongly influence the affairs of the business even after 1969 when his son-in-law had succeeded him as President. Crucially his own elevation to Chairman of the Board, had also meant the company's industrial relations remained heavily influenced by his own informal and easy manner and unionization remained off the agenda. In short, for all the discussions and changes that were captured by the 1975 documentary, the real power and decision-making had remained in the hands of Sam Steinberg and in important areas like industrial relations, the workforce recognized his hand at the wheel. So, when Sam Steinberg passed away unexpectedly, and his successors could not match his adept handling of the workforce, his absence led quickly to unionization which placed the company at a competitive disadvantage whilst the decentralized decision-making structure which he had introduced and had watched over proved unable to fill the leadership vacuum created by his passing.

Clearly the Steinberg case is instructive in pointing to succession planning not being limited to identifying an individual successor for a specific job. If it is to be effective it must look at decision-making and the exercise of power in a broader sense and must also include any specific elements of the company's strategy or policies or operations or relations with key counterparties, that are heavily influenced by the current generation and the next generation needs to deal with. To take account of Sam Steinberg's own words, the objective of succession planning must be the passing of the baton from one individual or one generation to another in such a way that a new driving force can take the company forward. And looking at press coverage of the company in 1950, nearly a decade after the passing of the matriarch founder Ida Steinberg, (This is How Mamma planned it) https://archive.macleans.ca/article/1950/7/15/this-is-how-mamma-planned-it, when the younger Sam Steinberg was rapidly expanding the family business, the values of the original matriarch founder, particularly the emphasis on giving customers more than they expected, were still very much in evidence in how Sam Steinberg and his brothers ran the business and were themselves willing to acknowledge the link between their success and their mothers' mantra. So, succession planning must not only concern itself with the identity of the individuals who will take on the baton from an earlier generation, but also with the transmission of values which will allow the new holder of the baton to be as effective at being a driving force for the good of the family business.

4.3.1.2. The Gucci family losing control of the Gucci luxury brand

The sale of the Steinberg business and the demise of the brand did not affect the Steinberg family's wealth and standing. In Gucci's case, the family experienced quite the opposite as the brand has thrived after the company relinquished control following a disastrous succession.

In 1921 Guccio Gucci, back in Florence after a stint working at the Savoy Hotel in London, opened a leather goods shop and focused initially at selling practical yet stylish leather luggage. By 1925, Guccio's three sons (Rodolfo, Vasco and Aldo) were also involved in the family business and gradually the product line was broadened to include shoes, belts and handbags. Innovations like the use of alternative materials in light of the trade embargo imposed on Italy after Italy's invasion of Ethiopia and inventing their own tanning technique that gave the Gucci leathers a distinctive feel allowed the Guccis to position their family business as creative trendsetters in the luxury goods industry. In 1938, Aldo persuaded his father to open a shop in Rome and after the war, with Guccio Gucci distributing his shares equally to his three sons in 1947, the brothers led by Aldo embarked on an internationalization drive establishing stores in New York, London and Paris. With the passing of Vasco without children, the family business ended up being a two brothers' affair with Rodolfo and Aldo at the helm and sharing equally the ownership of the business.

The first signs of trouble appeared when Giorgio Gucci, son of Aldo, who was a designer, launched his own Gucci Boutique brand outside the family business in 1969. Though this was reabsorbed in 1972, the first cracks between the two branches of the family had appeared. Subsequently, Paolo Gucci, Giorgio's brother, went on to launch Gucci Plus outside the family business after being blocked by the family in his efforts to launch a more accessible line of Gucci products within the family business. The family, including his father Aldo, used their leverage with suppliers to undermine Paolo's venture and he eventually abandoned the effort. Aldo's own direct ownership of Gucci America which had been used for the international expansion also became contentious but the tensions within the family were defused by consolidating Gucci America into the family-controlled Gucci Group in 1982 and turning the consolidated group into a publicly traded company.

The death of Rodolfo in 1983, marked a very open and public conflict between Rodolfo's son Maurizio on one side and his uncle Aldo on the other as they clashed on the direction of the business. Paradoxically, whilst the elder family members had been blocking Paolo's efforts of creating a more accessible Gucci line, in the 1980s the Gucci name was becoming almost ubiquitous on many products through licensing deals. Whilst the licensing generated short-term profits that were welcomed by Aldo, Maurizio was concerned that licensing was eroding the aura of exclusivity that Gucci had historically cultivated and damaging the Gucci brand in the long-term. During protracted legal battles that lasted till 1989, Maurizio leveraged Paolo's desire for his own line under the Gucci brand, to obtain and release evidence of tax evasion by Paolo's father Aldo, who ended up convicted and serving a year in prison in the US (1986). Aldo responded in kind with information sent to

Italian authorities on alleged inheritance tax evasion by Maurizio, who fled to Switzerland. Eventually, Maurizio prevailed in this family feud and in 1989 his uncle and his sons sold their part of the business to private equity group Investcorp who supported Maurizio's vision for the Gucci group.

Once in control, Maurizio brought in Dawn Mello in 1989, as Executive Vice President and chief designer, who trimmed the 1000+ stores down to 180 stores worldwide and reduced the items sold from 22,000 to 7,000 in a clear attempt to restore the sense of exclusivity. Dawn also revived two classic designs from earlier years – the Bamboo bag and the Gucci loafer shoe. But the turnaround was taking time and the company remained in the red during 1991 to 1993 with Maurizio being blamed for lavish spending at the group's headquarters in Florence and in Milan. In 1993, Maurizio sold the family's remaining 50% stake to Investcorp for a reported $190 million.

In the meantime, Dawn Mello had brought in Tom Ford who was named Creative Director in 1994. With Ford's creativity and Domenico De Sole's commercial acumen, Gucci's fortunes revived strongly and during the period 1995 to 1997, Investcorp sold its stake in Gucci for $1.9 billion. By 2019, there were 540 Gucci stores worldwide and global sales exceeded €9.6 billion and profits exceeded €3.9 billion. Today, Gucci remains a much admired and one of the most valuable luxury brands in the portfolio of Kering Group, but the Gucci family has no association or financial interest in the brand.

Clearly the transition from the generation of Aldo and Rodolfo to their children was a traumatic experience. But, perhaps the seeds of the break were already sown by Aldo's direct ownership of Gucci America which was after all leveraging the Gucci family name to build a separate business activity. Perhaps further seeds were sown with the reluctance of the older generation to allow the younger ones room to experiment under the family umbrella. Whilst Giorgio remained a creative influence, Paolo's idea of introducing a more accessible and affordable line under the family umbrella, was blocked but others like Armani and Valentino subsequently showed there was room for such lines as they launched their own affordable lines with Emporio Armani and Valentino Garavani with significant success. Overall, succession planning does not appear to have ever been a priority for the two brothers and in the end the family's feuding ended costing the family control of the family business.

4.3.1.3. Family relationships, mentoring and succession planning

We have already examined succession planning as an important element of Family Governance and reviewed the process that a family should consider in preparing for succession. And we have seen in the preceding examples how absence of succession planning (Gucci) and succession gone wrong (Steinberg) can impact the fortunes of a family business and those of the controlling family. The last area to address in relation to succession planning is the role that family relationships and mentoring can play in enhancing the prospects of a successful succession from one generation to the next.

It is clear that any selection process and any planning process for a leadership transition needs to take into account the state of the family business and its prospects. And it needs to take into account what a prospective candidate for the job can actually bring and not what they may learn on the job. This may help explain in part why in many parts of the world there is a strong belief that in family businesses the first generation establishes the business, the second generation grows it and the third generation often closes it or sells it.

Establishing a business is an entrepreneurial endeavour and requires a special type of resilience, drive and commitment to certain values and vision. The second generation is usually present for at least part of the journey of the founding entrepreneur and very often also participates in an apprentice like fashion in the family business. They witness first hand the struggles and sacrifices of the founding generation and may share in them too. The founding generation's resilience, drive and commitment to specific values and vision, very often come to also influence very heavily the second generation. As the family business becomes more established with the founder still at the helm, the second generation begins to have opportunities that the founder generation before them did not have. More formal education, including sometimes in business, wider networking opportunities, greater awareness of markets and technologies, greater financial means are some of the tools that a second generation of a successful family business very often has at their disposal that were not available to the founder entrepreneur. In such circumstances, a second generation can grow the family business including very often by some combination of diversification, integration and internationalization.

In contrast to the second generation's first-hand experiences of the family business and the family's own efforts to build the business, by the time the third generation becomes aware of the family business, the growth of the business may obstruct the struggles and the sacrifices of the founder and second generation from view. Whilst the third generation undoubtedly will have many tools that the second generation also benefited from and possibly more, they will inevitably always be short of first-hand experience of the early years, the early struggles and will not have experienced the resilience, drive and commitment to values and vision of the founder entrepreneur in the same way. Whilst they may still have the opportunity to join the family business and work their way up the ladder, the strength of the business and its viability is usually not in the balance as when the second generation had taken over. An element of consolidation and stewardship may in fact be required but will the third generation be best placed to provide that type of leadership? In such a scenario different skills and mindsets might be needed than the second generation's risk taking and growth seeking. But if the third generation has apprenticed at the feet of the second generation, they may be conditioned as well as predisposed to try and emulate their predecessors.

Timing the succession and phasing the succession appears to have the potential to impact the likelihood of a successful transition from one generation to the next. Allowing the next generation to experiment in a controlled manner either inside or outside the family business setting can help the next generation cut its teeth without risking the very existence of the family business. Passing the reins to the next generation whilst there is still some more building to do may be a better way to ensure the third generation's energies are productively utilized than letting them wait till the palace is completed and risking their desire to make their mark causes them to inadvertently bet or burn the palace down. In the corporate world, a former CEO is meant to be out of sight. In a family setting, can a family member truly step down from the family business? Even if they are giving the reins to the next generation, will they resist the temptation to meddle? In fact Family Governance institutions like the Family Council and the Family Assembly do provide the possibility for the earlier generations to remain involved in a constructive and not meddlesome way in the affairs of the family, including the family business, but discreetly and without undermining the position and authority of the later generations as they take charge of the family business.

4.4. Growth, internationalization, integration and diversification in the context of Family Governance

Growth, internationalization, vertical integration, horizontal integration and diversification are well known strategy dimensions over which Boards of companies and owners of companies exercise their judgment, often with the assistance of strategy consultants. Thus it may appear somewhat odd to discuss these dimensions of strategy in the context of Family Governance. At the same time, these dimensions can open up strategic options that a well-functioning Family Governance can leverage to the benefit of both the family business and the family itself.

One of the challenges that many family businesses face is that as the family members expand in numbers, the original family business cannot support them all. If we take one of the most common type of family businesses, the family-run restaurant founded by a matriarch or a patriarch of a family, it is very common that it can provide a nice standard of living for the matriarch's or patriarch's family whilst their children are relatively young. But when the children form families of their own, the same restaurant will not be able to provide the same standard of living to all the families of the two generations unless there is only one child in the second generation, or if only one child from the second generation gets involved in the business. For many families this is a non-issue as the children are not interested in the family business. But, for the families where the children are not only interested but also talented and committed to continue in the family business, growing the original family business can be the best way forward. In the restaurant example, opening further restaurants could lead to not only maintaining the two generations' standard of living but also improving it, as the single restaurant turns into a chain of restaurants by leveraging additional skills and talents that the second generation can bring to bear for such an expansion. Staying with the restaurant sector, vertical integration can offer another avenue for expansion. An example of diversification, integration and expansion that served both the business and the family well, is the well-known seafood business Legal Sea Foods, not only headquartered in Boston but a truly veritable Boston institution. According to the timewave on the Legal Sea Foods restaurant placemats, Henry Berkowitz opened a grocery store in Cambridge, Massachusetts in 1904. When grocery store chains like Stop & Shop began to enter the market in the late 1940s, George Berkowitz, Henry's son, opened a fish market adjacent to his father's grocery store in 1950 and called it Legal Fish Market. This diversification allowed customers to buy groceries and fish in essentially one location and gave fresh impetus to the family business. Legal Fish Market offered fresh fish and cooked fish and chips to go. In 1968, the family opened a restaurant in the space adjacent to their stores and offered a simple menu with fish and chips, fried clams, fried shrimp and fried scallops on simple paper plates. This forward integration brought the family into the restaurant business where their commitment to freshness and quality differentiated them and became a lasting source of competitive advantage. In 1975, the family business expanded to two restaurants and in 1981, its clam chowder was served at President Reagan's inauguration, starting a bipartisan tradition still going strong. The same year, the family's commitment to the tagline of its business, "If it ain't fresh it ain't legal" was confirmed through the establishment of their own Legal Quality Control Center for fish processing and distribution, thereby turning Legal Sea Foods into an industry leader in food safety and public health. In 1992, Roger Berkowitz, George's son and active in the business since the age of ten, took over the reins of the family business. Under his leadership it expanded significantly and at the start of the Covid pandemic the business had annualized revenues in excess of $200 million and operated 33 locations that included different formats and menus and integrated fresh fish retailing at its larger locations. In December 2020, in response to the pandemic, Legal Sea Foods was sold to PPX Hospitality Brands, a subsidiary of Danu Partners. Under the terms of the sale, Berkowitz keeps control of online and retail sales using the Legal Sea Foods name and PPX are the new owners of the restaurant locations and the Quality Control Center in Boston. For over 100 years and three generations, the Berkowitz family has been successful in the food retailing sector, and even though its market focus has been transformed more than once through diversification and integration, successive generations of Berkowitz leaders have driven the family business forward on essentially the same commitment to freshness and quality in the interest of the customer.

Internationalization is another strategic option that later generations have historically been adept at utilizing to expand family businesses. We have already seen the example of Gucci. Being given the opportunity to grow a business internationally can be a very good way to give the family members of the next generations the opportunity to cut their teeth and prove their mettle as leaders in a way that has limited downside, provided the resources utilized in such expansion are carefully rationed and monitored, and very significant upside. When such internationalization efforts are successful, they have the potential to transform the original business, particularly as very often the new markets are significantly bigger than the market of the original business. In parallel, by proving themselves in new markets, the leaders of the next generation prove themselves as worthy of taking over in very clear and motivating ways. Their subsequent ascent to leadership roles for the entire family business become more legitimate and are perceived as earned as opposed to driven by connection to the family.

4.5. Chapter closing thoughts

Family Governance is vital in regulating the affairs of the family and the family's interactions with the business in ways that enhance the prospects of longevity for the family business. Clearly the absence of Family Governance reduces the prospects of a family business remaining under the control of the founding family beyond its third generation.

Chapter 5:
Interrelationship between Corporate and Family Governance

5.1. Overlapping and complementary nature of Corporate and Family Governance

We have examined in some detail Corporate Governance and Family Governance. They each require structures and policies to be introduced and each aim to regulate relationships and decision-making. This is hardly surprising given they are both forms of governance. In order for each of them to work well, the principal actors involved in each form of governance need to be committed to taking their roles and duties seriously. When they do work well, each form of governance has a positive impact on the prospects of the family business. When each form is absent or poorly applied, either on its own or together with the other, the family business is impacted in a negative way. Again, this is hardly surprising since the forms of governance have purposes with considerable overlaps.

As we have seen, Corporate Governance aims to protect and promote the interests of the business and those of its shareholders. Family Governance aims to promote both the interests of the family and the interests of the family business. Hence, to a degree both Corporate Governance and Family Governance cover the same ground from different angles or similar ground from the same angles. We have seen how succession planning is an important part of good Corporate Governance, but we have also examined its importance for and how integral a part it is of, Family Governance in a family business. Both cover the same ground but from different angles. On the other hand, what is the nature of the oversight body that oversees management is an example where similar ground, is covered from the same perspective by both Corporate and Family Governance. In the case of Corporate Governance, the need of oversight of management is met through the Board of Directors or similar body which is accountable to the shareholders and the method by which such a Board of Directors is elected by the shareholders is usually a matter of law, listing requirement or regulation. In the case of Family Governance, the need for oversight of management in a family business is addressed by the oversight body but also influenced by the preferences of the family which determines the nature and composition of the oversight body via the interaction between the Family Institutions.

Figure 5.1.a. Interrelationship between Corporate and Family Governance

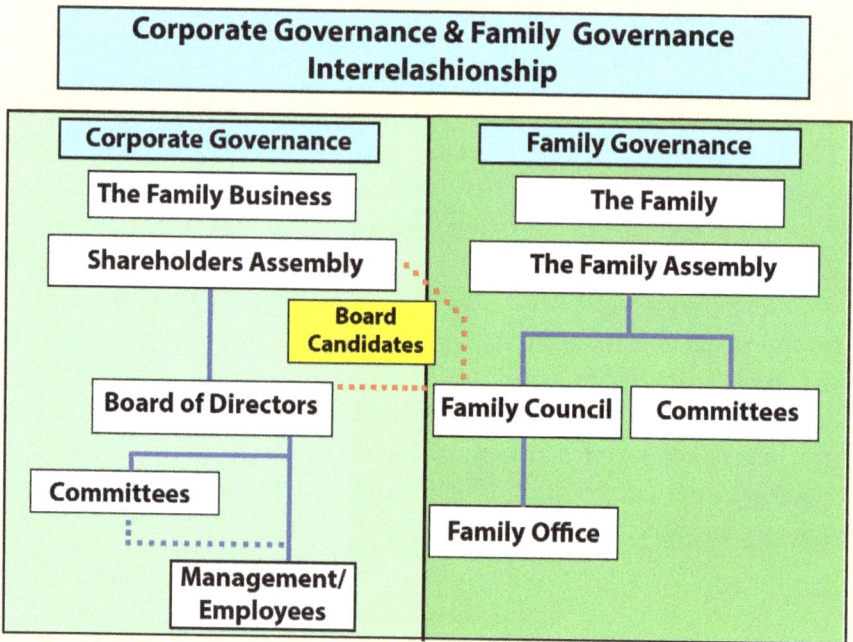

5.2. Value of Corporate Governance and Family Governance when seeking external finance

Many businesses fund their growth through internally generated funds but many more businesses also use capital, debt or equity or both, that is provided by external capital providers. Access to such external finance can be a critical success factor or an accelerating factor. All providers of external finance have their own ways of assessing risk and determining whether to become a lender or an equity investor in a business. But the information they all seek is essentially the same and intended to provide answers to questions that include among others:

- ✓ What is the business model of the company? Is it sustainable and profitable?
- ✓ How competitive is the company and how sustainable is its market position? What risks and threats does the company face in its business and how does it deal with these?
- ✓ What is the market environment in which the business operates? Are there any positive or negative trends to be mindful of?
- ✓ How capable and experienced is the company's Board, management and leadership? How deep is the management and leadership bench of the company?
- ✓ What is the strategy of the company? Does it seem achievable given its position, resources at its disposal including management and leadership and market environment?
- ✓ How will the funds to be provided be used by the business?
- ✓ Is the company complying with tax and regulatory requirements? Are there any issues, challenges or risks with respect to tax, environmental and other regulatory requirements that can impact the business?
- ✓ In the case of loans, the 3Cs (character, cashflow, collateral) of credit assessment translate to how likely are the owners/managers of the business to repay the loans and will the business be able to generate sufficient cashflow to repay the loans? Is there any collateral that can secure the borrowings?
- ✓ In the case of equity, how will the value of the business grow to enable a return on the equity investment? And what will be the liquidity events that will allow the returns to be crystallized?

Perhaps not surprisingly, since external capital providers are in essence facing an asset allocation decision, most if not all the questions above are also the preoccupation of a company's Board of Directors and senior management. Moreover, as we have seen up till now, the way most of these questions are addressed by individual Boards and senior management teams are linked with the nature of Corporate Governance and Family Governance prevalent in their businesses. It is therefore not surprising that family businesses with good Corporate Governance and effective Family Governance can answer such questions more readily and more convincingly than family businesses which have neither. In fact, some external finance providers consider the Corporate Governance and

Family Governance practiced by prospective counterparties as an important part of their due diligence in two specific ways. Firstly, in terms of what the presence or absence of such governance signals with respect to the commitment of the owners and managers of the business to the principles of governance and its components such as succession planning and shareholder rights. Secondly, family businesses that have adopted good Corporate Governance and Family Governance are much more likely to provide information flows that lenders and investors value and want to see since they already have them for their own use.

Overall, good Corporate Governance and Family Governance facilitate a wider access to capital at better terms for the family businesses with such governance in place. When family businesses with both good Corporate Governance and Family Governance are listed, their rating is enhanced and their valuations are more generous.

5.3. Interaction of Corporate and Family Governance when listing the family business on a stock exchange

Listing the shares of a family business on a stock exchange is a very important and generally irreversible step in the evolution of a family business. It deserves careful consideration and we examine the advantages and disadvantages of taking such a step and the preparations that are advisable for it. It is important to note that once a family decides to list the family business on a stock exchange, it is no longer the only stakeholder in determining the future of the business and the Corporate Governance for the business. Every stock exchange has rules and regulations that listed companies need to observe in order to attain and maintain listed status. Hence, the family considering a listing needs to reconcile itself and be comfortable with the fact that as a listed company, their family business which they may still control after the listing depending on the terms of their initial public offering (IPO), has to comply with the exchange's rules and regulations.

5.3.1. Pros and cons for listing a family business on a stock exchange

5.3.1.1. Advantages of going public for a family business

A public offering of shares of a company to investors allows the company issuing the shares to receive an injection of equity capital which it can use in whichever way the Board of the issuing company sees fit. This sale of shares by the company dilutes the shareholding of the existing family shareholders. Consequently, it is in the interest of the family shareholders that the price at which the shares of the family business are offered is higher rather than lower, as it will mean correspondingly lower instead of higher dilution, i.e. decrease, of the family's shareholding in the listed family business.

Listing shares on a stock exchange improves the marketability of the shares and this is perhaps the most obvious advantage or benefit from a listing of the shares of the family business. The possibility to sell shares or use shares as collateral for loans can address liquidity needs for shareholders preferring to hold their wealth in assets other than their interest in the family company. The liquidity that a listing confers on the shares allows individual family members to monetize some or all of their shareholdings in the family business.

The liquidity of the shares of a listed family business offers another advantage for a family business as it becomes a more attractive place to work for ambitious and capable non-family managers, since their compensation can also include options on these liquid shares. In such circumstances, a non-family professional manager can have a direct and simple mechanism for monetizing any shares they accumulate in the listed business. By comparison, a professional manager who is not a family member, even if granted some shares in a privately-held family business, will not be able to monetize their interest in the family business very easily. Thus, a listing can enhance the pool of senior management talent that the family business can draw from.

Another advantage arising from a listing is an increase in the value of the shares that is due to them becoming readily negotiable, i.e. capable of being sold quickly through the market, as well as due to the fact public companies meet higher transparency standards which can underpin higher valuation for the shares. Compliance with the listing requirements of the stock exchange, which includes adhering to the exchange's guidelines on Corporate Governance, increases investors' confidence in the company and its reported financial performance and by extension the demand for and price for its shares.

A further advantage can be an improved ability to access debt financing on better terms as a public company with a market capitalization which is significantly higher than the accounting value of the equity in the business.

As public companies have to publish financial statements and performance data as well as offer analysts the opportunity to put questions to the company's senior management on a set cycle set by the exchange (e.g. in the US the major exchanges require quarterly reporting), the investing public tends to perceive public companies, with some justification, as more transparent and potentially also more professionally managed. The requirement for communications to shareholders and analysts imposed by the exchanges thus increases the visibility of the company and improves its perceived standing.

5.3.1.2. Disadvantages of going public for a family business

As we have already seen, public companies have to comply with the relevant exchange rules on communications to shareholders and possibly other stakeholders and these communications are generally much more frequent than for privately-held companies. Consequently, one of the disadvantages from going public is a relative loss of privacy since as a listed company, the family business will have to communicate and explain detailed financial statements and other performance measures as well as any advantages given to family members, either as managers or shareholders.

In addition to a loss of privacy, a listing also means a loss of complete autonomy for the shareholding family. Under the rules of every reputable stock exchange, every shareholder is guaranteed certain basic rights. As a result the introduction of new shareholders in the ownership structure of a listed family company means that even when such new shareholders comprise the minority, they still have rights that mean family members can no longer operate completely unfettered. Indeed the shareholding family will need to respect such minority shareholder rights. Consequently, a family controlling a business should only seek a listing for the shares of its family business, if it is unconcerned with this particular disadvantage or considers it is a reasonable limitation the family can live with given the advantages and benefits conferred by such a listing.

A listed family company also carries greater liability risk than a privately-held family business, in relation to information they provide to its non-family shareholders. For example erroneous financial reporting can lead to litigation against the company.

A further potential disadvantage arising from a listing, depending on the proportion of the shares that end up being held by non-family members, is that a listed company can be taken over. Thus, if enough shares are issued to outsiders it could lead to external investors gaining control over the family business.

Of course, a final disadvantage from a listing are the substantial one-off costs associated with going public (e.g. registration costs at the exchange, legal fees, underwriters' commission) as well as the ongoing reporting and compliance costs.

5.3.2. Preparation for listing a family business on a stock exchange

An IPO raises capital for the family business and places a value on the company by selling newly issued shares to external investors, including sophisticated institutional investors and retail investors. Such an IPO is a combination of selling and marketing the company's story and prospect within specified regulatory parameters. Going public is a long and complex process and requires specialist professional advice and help, including with respect to legal issues, financial and marketing communications to investors. A family preparing for a listing of its family business should always keep in mind that investors are willing to pay more for companies that can demonstrate a long-term track record of good Corporate Governance practices before the actual IPO and three areas stand out in this respect

✓ Shareholder Rights
✓ Board of Directors
✓ Transparency and Disclosure

In each of these areas, there are best practices which the family should seek to adhere to ahead of an IPO.

In respect of shareholder rights, best practices ahead of IPO that the family should be aware of and adhere to would include:

- ✓ Ensuring clear protection of minority shareholders in charter, bylaws and company governance code irrespective of actual local legal requirement – meeting a higher standard than what is legally required is one of the most powerful ways for a family business to stand out and gain investor confidence ahead of an IPO
- ✓ Providing adequate notice for shareholder meetings and sharing the agenda of all shareholders' meetings with all shareholders
- ✓ Granting the ability to all shareholders to participate and vote meaningfully at a shareholders' meetings (e.g. cumulative voting for directors) – ideally also providing the ability to shareholders to call meetings and add agenda items provided certain voting thresholds are reached
- ✓ Treating shareholders fairly regarding information disclosure including in respect of material agreements with specific shareholders, conflicts of interest etc.
- ✓ Being clear about the rights of different classes of shares if more than one class of shares exists – investors understand the difference between voting rights and economic rights and may accept fewer voting rights if they are confident their economic rights will be respected.

In respect of Board of Directors, best practices ahead of IPO that the family should be aware of and adhere to would include:

- ✓ Having the right mix of professional skills (e.g. marketing, strategy, international financial markets, accounting and audit committee expertise) around the Board table, always with reference to the family business industry and market segment
- ✓ Having a strong independent component in the composition of the Board – it is critical that the Board is not perceived as simply friends of the founder or the family
- ✓ Separating the chairman and CEO roles
- ✓ Regulating schedule and agenda of Board meetings
- ✓ Having Board committees responsible for oversight in certain key areas (e.g. audit, governance, nominations, and remuneration)
- ✓ Initial and continuous director education
- ✓ Periodic evaluation of directors

In respect of transparency and disclosure, best practices ahead of IPO that the family should be aware of and adhere to would include:

- ✓ Ensuring information is prepared and disclosed in accordance with high quality standards of accounting, financial and nonfinancial disclosure
- ✓ Annual audit conducted by an independent, competent and qualified auditor in accordance with International Auditing Standards or other relevant prevailing standards
- ✓ Engaging reputable external auditors who are accountable to the shareholders and exercise due professional care in the conduct of the audit
- ✓ Establishing channels for disseminating information that could provide equal, timely and cost-efficient access to relevant information by users (e.g. Investor Relations section as part of the company's online presence)

Essentially, listing requires Corporate Governance that meets at least the standards laid down by the exchange. A good listing requires good Corporate Governance which meets and exceeds such standards. So, in a family business, the listing preparations include introducing and implementing Corporate Governance. Indeed, Corporate Governance becomes a precondition for achieving the goal of listing and in order to do that you also need Family Governance. So overall, in order for a controlling family to consider a listing for its family business, it needs to introduce and practice both Family Governance with respect to the family and Corporate Governance with respect to the family business company.

5.4. Benefits from combination of Corporate Governance and Family Governance

There are multiple benefits from the combination of Corporate Governance and Family Governance. Some are driven from the Corporate Governance side and some from the Family Governance side, and some from both.

- ✓ Family Governance contributes to achieving a united family and allows the family to speak with one voice. Given how disunity can destroy values and families, this is a very important benefit for both the family and the business. In respect of the business, the unity that Family Governance promotes can have a profoundly positive effect on the Corporate Governance of the family business, since the family acts and speaks in a united way as owners of the business

✓ By requiring collective involvement from family members and prescribing the mechanisms for such involvement, Family Governance also legitimizes family leaders and their decisions and actions. Once again, this has a very positive effect on Corporate Governance since the family leaders' interaction with the business is also legitimized in this way

✓ Family Governance also provides a mechanism for obtaining support from passive members of the family who are not directly involved in the family business in any way, by respecting their rights and regulating their potential exits rather than preventing such exits. This reduces the likelihood of intrafamily conflict and consequently is also beneficial for the family business since intrafamily conflicts, especially when centred around ownership and the future direction of the family business can be both distracting and destructive

✓ As Family Governance provides a forum for the family shareholders and improves communications within the family and between the family business and the family members, it ensures less interference in the business itself

✓ One of the biggest benefits arising from Family Governance is that it facilitates the integration of incoming generations by providing clear transitional arrangements as well as mentoring and training opportunities. And through the Family Council, it ensures deliberate rather than random inclusion

✓ Another benefit comes from the clarity that Family Governance can provide on family employment within the family business through the Family's Employment Policies. These policies set clear employment criteria and eliminate entitlement or silo mentality

✓ Finally, Family Governance also provides a framework for the management of conflict by establishing protocols which provide clarity and set rules facilitating internal conflict resolution

✓ Corporate Governance on the other hand benefits family businesses by improving the family's understanding of ownership and management issues. This is accomplished through clear delineation of the responsibilities of the owners and the managers and formalizing the communication between owners and managers.

✓ Corporate Governance also provides clarity to the management of the family business as it helps clarify the owners' objectives and their requirements on risk and returns and helps set guidelines for management's actions and decisions.

✓ Corporate Governance and Family Governance also provides clarity to the owning family as they crystallize commitment to the business and the family via policies, via the constitution and via institutions as well as set rules on how to deal with issues and take ownership decisions.

✓ And as we have already seen, external capital providers, both lenders and investors place a premium on Corporate and Family Governance. So, one of the key benefits from the adoption of both good Corporate Governance and Family Governance, is the family business has more options to fund the growth of the business as it can draw funds from a wider pool of capital and on better terms.

Figure 5.4.a. Main benefits from Corporate and Family Governance

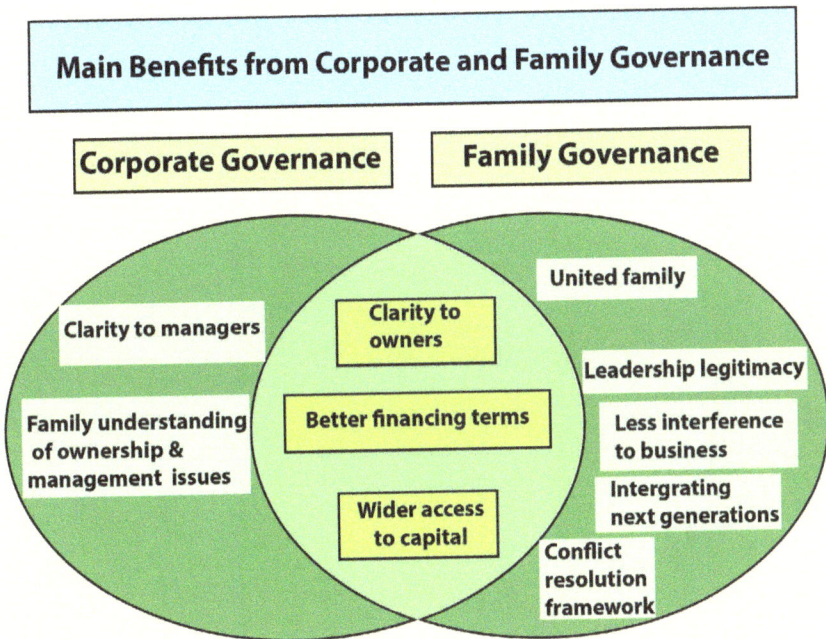

Main Benefits from Corporate and Family Governance

Corporate Governance   **Family Governance**

United family

Clarity to managers

Clarity to owners

Leadership legitimacy

Family understanding of ownership & management issues

Better financing terms

Less interference to business

Intergrating next generations

Wider access to capital

Conflict resolution framework

As can be seen from the above, all the different benefits that arise from Corporate and Family Governance are fundamentally enhancing the prospects of longevity for the family business as they create more sustainable, healthy and clear relationships and interactions between the family and the family business, between the family members themselves and between the family and the management of the family business. It is therefore not an accident that the few family businesses which survive past third generation, are generally characterized by good Corporate Governance and Family Governance which insulates the family business from any issues arising within the family.

5.5. Chapter closing thoughts

The twin pillars of Corporate Governance and Family Governance are necessary though not sufficient conditions by themselves, for a family business to become multigenerational. Good Corporate Governance and Family Governance are the two disciplines that carry family businesses across generations.

Annex 1:
Sample areas for ICQs

- ➢ Mission
- ➢ Planning
- ➢ Control Environment
- ➢ Monitoring Overall Performance
- ➢ Effectiveness of Processes
- ➢ Efficiency of Processes
- ➢ Allocation of Resources
- ➢ Use of Resources
- ➢ Operating Environment: Compliance with Laws & Regulations
- ➢ Operating Environment: Compatibility with External Environment
- ➢ Budgetary Controls & Follow up Reviews
- ➢ Cash & Cheque Receipts
- ➢ Payments
- ➢ Cash on Hand & in Banks
- ➢ Deposits to Company Treasury
- ➢ Cash Funds
- ➢ Investments
- ➢ Revenue Enhancement, Market Trends & Updates
- ➢ Cost Recovery: Allocation & Apportionment
- ➢ Billing to Customers
- ➢ Accounts Receivables
- ➢ Inventory: Goods, Materials & Stores
- ➢ Operating Fixed Assets
- ➢ Purchasing & Payables
- ➢ Payroll
- ➢ Human Resources Planning, Control & Management
- ➢ Financial Planning, Accounting & Reporting
- ➢ Services (include both to and by the company)
- ➢ Information System: Management & Controls

Annex 2:
Links to examples of Codes of Conduct

Alphabet (parent of Google)

https://abc.xyz/investor/other/code-of-conduct/

Apple – supplier

https://www.apple.com/supplier-responsibility/pdf/Apple-Supplier-Code-of-Conduct-and-Supplier-Responsibility-Standards.pdf

Astra-Zeneca

https://www.astrazeneca.com/content/dam/az/PDF/Sustainability/Code_of_Ethics_English.pdf

Coca-Cola

https://www.coca-colacompany.com/content/dam/journey/us/en/policies/pdf/corporate-governance/code-of-business-conduct/coca-cola-coc-external.pdf

Johnson & Johnson

https://www.jnj.com/_document?id=00000159-69fe-dba3-afdb-79ff-cdd60000

Microsoft Inc.

file:///C:/Users/CChristou/Downloads/Microsoft%20SBC%20-%20English.pdf

Nestle

https://www.nestle.com/sites/default/files/asset-library/documents/library/documents/corporate_governance/code_of_business_conduct_en.pdf

Starbucks

https://globalassets.starbucks.com/assets/eecd184d6d2141d58966319744393d1f.pdf

Toyota

https://www.toyota-global.com/pages/contents/company/vision_philosophy/pdf/code_of_conduct.pdf

Unilever

https://www.unilever.com/Images/code-of-business-principles-and-code-policies_tcm244-409220_en.pdf

Annex 3: Family Governance Summary Checklist

	Question	Yes	No	Comment
1	Is it clear to all concerned who is a member of the family with respect to the business in question?			
2	Are all members of the family actively involved in the running of the business?			
3	Does the family have formal governance arrangements in place intended to ensure long term business continuity and family harmony?			
4	Does the family have rules regarding the family's engagement with the family-controlled business?			
5	If there are rules regarding the family's engagement with the family-controlled business are they part of a formal and broader family constitution governing how family members interact with the business and with each other with respect to the business?			
6	Does the family have a family Board or other governance structure in place?			
7	Are the activities of the family Board (if it exists) or other governance structure formalized in any document?			
8	Does the family have a set of policies relating to its relationship with the family-controlled companies?			
9	Are there clear rules for family members who work in family-controlled companies?			
10	Is there a clear separation of the roles between the Family Council and the Board of Directors of the family-controlled company?			

11	Is there a separate organization and structure outside the family-controlled business in place to manage family wealth and other issues (i.e. a Family Office)?			
12	Are personal expenses, investments or other personal services handled outside the family-controlled company?			
13	Does the family have a charity or foundation or engage in other non-profit activities in an organized manner?			
14	Does the family have mechanisms in place aimed at continuity in either the ownership or management or both of the family in the business?			

Annex 4: An Example of a Family Employment Policy prioritizing the needs of the Family Business

Employment philosophy

The driving force behind human resource decisions should be the best interest of the organization and not that of individual family member(s)

1. Attract the most qualified people, both family and non-family
2. A job with the business is neither a birthright nor an obligation for family members
3. Once hired, family members will be treated as all other non-family employees
4. No guarantee that family employees will be promoted to senior management positions, simply because they are part of the family
5. Family employees are expected to set the example in terms of dedication, performance and conduct
6. Cannot and will not carry individuals, whether family members or not, who do not make a full contribution

Existence of an open position

1. The business must have a position available for which the applying family member is suitably qualified
2. The business will not create a position for a family member unless the growth of the business justifies it, which is to be decided by the company's Board
3. Non-family employees will not be dismissed to make room for family members

Prerequisite qualifications

1. Educational requirements: a university degree or other appropriate academic qualification from a reputable university/institution is required for employment in any position within the company
2. Outside work experience: Successful working experience of 3–5 years is welcome though not always required. In cases of no prior work experience, new family employees to undergo "initial training" of 6–12 months aiming at:
   - Introducing them and exposing them to the company
   - Helping them validate their professional interests
   - Allowing the company to assess them
3. Age Limit: The business should not be considered a "shelter" for family members in search of a job. Hence, for any family member aged 40+ interested to join for first time, the Board will examine their professional career path and their reasons for not joining earlier

Family employment specifics

1. Family members who wish to join the business should inform the CEO and complete standard application materials
2. Family members will go through the standard interviewing, assessment and selection process
3. Final decision for hiring or rejecting a family candidate rests with the Board of the company
4. Once a family member becomes an employee, he/she will be treated as any other non-family employee. Family employees will be trained, supervised, evaluated and promoted like other employees
5. Family employees will have regular performance reviews through standard channels and will be given feedback on their performance and guidance on how they might improve like all employees. Additionally, their performance will be reviewed at corporate level for possible guidance/action in relation to their prospective career plans within the company
6. In order to contribute to the development and advancement of family members, a "Development Plan" will be elaborated for every family member. This plan would encompass training, continuing education, coaching, mentoring, special projects and assignments, job rotations etc.

7. As part of their performance management and self-assessment, family employees will be asked to provide a yearly self-assessment, including personal development objectives for the following year

8. In respect of promotion of family members, a recommendation will be made by their supervisor or by the company's management with the final decision being taken by the Board

9. Grounds for dismissing a family member include continued poor performance, unacceptable personal conduct or breach of company's ethics, and any other grounds on which a non-family employee may be dismissed

10. If dismissed a family member cannot be reconsidered for employment

11. If a family member voluntarily leaves, he/she may return to work with the business subject to the Board's approval if an appropriate position is vacant. This would generally be limited to one time only.

Compensation

1. Compensation and benefits of family employees will be based on their position, responsibilities, qualifications and performance and will be comparable to that on non-family employees in the same/similar position and with similar qualifications

2. Compensation and benefits will be based on being employees and not on the shares they own

Other family employment policies

1. In-laws' employment: family spouses wishing to join the business will go through the standard interviewing, assessment and selection process with final decision with the Board where the family member concerned would be excluded from voting and rest of Board would vote confidentially

2. Supervision and reporting relationships: wherever possible, family members will not be supervised by other family members but if unavoidable such situations should be approved and monitored by the Board

3. Short-term internships and summer employment: younger family members showing desire/interest to join the business will be encouraged to go through short-term internships with the business, but this

will not replace required initial training if they join full time at later stage

4. Continuing education: standard company policy will apply both to continuing education (for a degree) and to professional development (e.g. training, seminars, conferences). In case of a degree, the Family Council may sanction greater support than available to non-family members

www.ingramcontent.com/pod-product-compliance
Lightning Source LLC
Chambersburg PA
CBHW041144230326
41599CB00039BA/7171